TOURISM AND THE HOTEL AND CATERING INDUSTRIES IN THE EC

European Community Law Series
Series Editor: Professor D. Lasok, QC (University of Exeter)

European Community Law is having an important impact upon the law of the United Kingdom and other countries concerned with EC legislation. This new series provides authoritative and up-to-date accounts of specific topics and areas. The volumes are addressed to legal practitioners, in-house lawyers, businessmen and to all those who need to communicate with lawyers in this field.

Already published volumes include:
1 Peter Stone, *Copyright Law in the UK and the European Community*

2 Frank Wooldridge, *Company Law in the UK and the European Community*

3 Rosa Greaves, *Transport Law of the European Community*

4 Friedl Weiss, *Public Procurement in European Community Law*

5 A. J. Easson, *Taxation in the European Community*

Future volumes will include:
Philippe Bourin, *The European Investment Bank: Its Structure and Functions in Financing Community and Non-Community Projects*

David Freestone, *Environmental Protection in European Community Law*

Syamal Chatterjee, *Legal Aspects of Drug Control and Treatment of Drug-dependent Persons within the European Community*

Timothy Portwood, *Mergers in EC Competition Law*
Joint Ventures in EC Law

European Community Law Series

6

Tourism and the Hotel and Catering Industries in the EC

Frans van Kraay

THE ATHLONE PRESS
London & Atlantic Highlands, NJ

First published 1993 by The Athlone Press Ltd
1 Park Drive, London NW11 7SG and
165 First Avenue, Atlantic Highlands, NJ 07716

British Library Cataloguing in Publication Data
A catalogue record for this book is available
from the British Library
ISBN 0–485–70011–5

Library of Congress Cataloging in Publication Data
Van Kraay, Frans, 1944–
Tourism and the hotel and catering industries in the EC / Frans Van Kraay
p. cm. — (European Community law series: 6)
Includes bibliographical references and index.
ISBN 0–485–70011–5 (c) : £45.00 ($90.00 U.S.)
1. Tourist trade—Law and legislation—European Economic Community countries. 2. Hotels—Law and legislation—European Economic Community countries. 3. Caterers and catering—Law and legislation—European Economic Community countries. I. Title. II. Series.
KJE6825, V36 1993
343, 4'07864794—dc20
[344, 037864794] 93–7263
CIP

Typeset by Datix International Limited, Bungay, Suffolk
Printed and bound in Great Britain by University Press, Cambridge

Contents

Series Preface

West European integration has become an irreversible and ever-expanding process affecting directly not only the Member States of the European Community but also business interests and individuals in all walks of life. The prediction that, in time, 80 per cent of the national legislation will eventually emanate from Brussels may not be accurate but the volume of regulations and directives so far produced in the Community has already assumed formidable dimensions. Consequently textbooks, commentaries and source publications have grown in size to the point of being too voluminous to be handled by anyone interested in a particular area. Moreover, in view of the abundance of material, large publications cannot always do justice to every topic which merits treatment in depth.

In response to this challenge, The Athlone Press has launched a European Community Law Series addressed mainly to legal practice and the business world and also to students of law. The Series consists of concise and relatively short monographs designed to break new ground and fill the gaps in the existing literature. In monographs unencumbered with general information but still within the context of the integrative process, the Series offers guidance to the practitioner and businessman.

Volumes in the Series take more or less self-contained subjects, and the Series will eventually compose a specialist library.

D. Lasok

Series Editor

Volume Preface

This book aims to give an overview and analysis of the activities of the EC in the sphere of tourism. It not only outlines the initial objectives and themes of action in this sphere, but also deals with subjects such as the freedom of movement of tourists, the right of establishment, the freedom to provide services, the movement of capital relevant to tourism, and other matters of great practical importance to the tourist industry such as EC financial support for tourism.

The EC's actions undertaken to date are scrutinized and evaluated. These actions range from general internal market measures and actions resulting from EC policies to direct measures. Some actions of particular importance for business and consumers, such as package travel and developments in the hotel and catering sphere, are highlighted. Attention is also given to developments in the sphere of transfrontier property transactions. The latest EC action plan to supplement earlier achievements brings the picture up to date.

The main aim of the book is to bring together the great many achievements, plans, rules, laws and policies relevant to both tourists and the tourist industry and to provide those with an interest in tourism with a concise work on the subject covering all areas. At the time of writing it was unclear whether a policy on tourism would be formally incorporated into the Treaty of Maastricht but, unfortunately, this did not happen. For this and other reasons not much consolidation has as yet taken place: this book thus aims to contribute to the process of compilation and consolidation.

I am indebted to Professor D. Lasok, the Series Editor, who not only invited me to write the book in the first place but who set aside valuable time from his own pressing duties to guide me on certain parts of the work and who furnished me with valuable information. My thanks are also due to many others throughout Europe, who have given me assistance and provided recent information. I would like to mention, in particular, Professor Riccardo Monaco (until recently President of Unidroit and sometime Judge at the European Court of Justice); Professor Robert Pourvoyeur (Honorary Director General, EC Council of Ministers and Professor Emeritus at Antwerp University); Mr Edward McMillan Scott MEP, Professor Sergio Neri (former Director of research and documentation at the European Court of Justice); Dr Heinrich von Moltke (Director General of DG XXIII) and his staff, and staff of the information departments of virtually all the institutions of the European Communities, including the Economic and Social Committee.

Closer to home, I should like to thank John Chillag and his library staff at the Mid-Yorkshire European Information Centre and my wife Milena and son Theo for their patience and assistance in the typing and correcting process. Finally, I must express my gratitude to the Publishers, The Athlone Press, for their assistance all the way from the initial mooting of the idea of a book on tourism to its completion and publication.

I wish to acknowledge the support provided by the above and the assistance others have given me, but I remain of course solely responsible for the contents.

Frans van Kraay

List of Abbreviations

ABTA	The Association of British Travel Agents
ASOR	Accord Services Occasionels par Route
BC-Net	Business Cooperation Network
BEUC	Union of European Consumer Unions
BITS	International Office for Social Tourism
CAA	Civil Aviation Authority
CAP	Common Agricultural policy
CEDEFOP	Centre for the Development of Vocational Training
CIRCOM	Coopérative Internationale de Recherche et d'Action en matière de Communication
CMLR	Common Market Law Reports
CMLRev	*Common Market Law Review*
Dir.	Directive
EAGGF	European Agricultural Guidance and Guarantee fund
ECJ	European Court of Justice
EEC	European Economic Community
EEIG	European Economic Interest Grouping
EFTA	European Free Trade Association
EIB	European Investment Bank
ELRev	*European Law Review*
ENVIREG	Regional Action Programme concerning the Environment
ERDF	European Regional Development Fund
ESC	Economic and Social Committee
ETC	European Travel Commission
Euro-chambers	European Association of Chambers of Commerce and Industry
EYT	European Year of Tourism
FEEE	Foundation for Environmental Education in Europe
FORCE	Continuing vocational training programme

HORECA	Hotels, restaurants, and cafés sector
HOTREC	Confederation of National Hotel and Restaurant Associations in the EC
ICLQ	*International and Comparative Law Quarterly*
IHA	International Hotel Association
IMP's	Integrated Mediterranean Programmes
JALT	*Journal of the Association of Law Teachers*
LEADER	Link between Actions for the Development of the Rural Economy
LEDA	Local Employment Development Action research programme
NCI	New Community Instrument
OECD	Organisation for Economic Cooperation and Development
PHARE	Poland and Hungary, Aid for Economic Restructuring
Reg.	Regulation
SIS	Standard Information System
SMEs	Small and Medium-sized Enterprises
Supp	Supplement
UCITS	Undertakings for Collective Investment in Transferable Securities
Unidroit	International Institute for the Unification of Private Law
VVF	Villages Vacances Familles
WTO	World Tourism Organisation

1

Introduction

For some considerable time the European Community has been interested in the problems caused by tourism. The European Commission in particular has stressed the importance of tourism and considered how it related to other EC activities.[1] Article 2 of the EC Treaty indicated the importance of the promotion of closer relations between the Member States and it goes without saying that tourism can be of assistance to the EC in the achievement of this objective by bringing the citizens of Europe closer together.

THE IMPORTANCE OF TOURISM

The importance of tourism should be stressed in the context of the concept of a people's Europe. If organized properly, tourism could be one of the ways for EC citizens to get to know and understand each other better. Unfortunately, some forms of mass tourism have rather the opposite effect. Therefore it is essential that tourism is organized more effectively. The European Parliament has come out resolutely in favour of EC action to promote and develop it.[2]

The European Council, when it discussed a People's Europe in June 1984 and March 1985, asked the Institutions and other authorities to give special attention to tourism since it is of such importance to the people of Europe.[3] The Council of Ministers in 1984 emphasized the need to take the tourism dimension more fully into consideration in the decision-making process and asked the Commission to present its proposals on tourism based on consultations with the Member States.[4] The Council stressed that tourism is an important factor within the integration of Europe and that tourism affects and is affected by many of the EC's activities.

ECONOMIC IMPORTANCE

Tourism is also a significant economic activity within the meaning of Article 2 EEC and provides, labour intensive as it is, employment for 7.5 million people (i.e. 6 per cent of total employment). The Economic and Social Committee (ESC) estimates the figure as high as 10 million.[5] Tourism represents approximately 5.5 per cent of the EC's gross domestic product, 8 per cent of private consumption and 4.5 per cent of currency inflow and outflow.[6] There are however considerable differences between the Member States. Countries such as Spain, France, Greece, Italy and Portugal for obvious reasons derive a large net surplus from their tourist trade. In Ireland earnings are slightly higher than expenditure, while in Belgium, Denmark, Germany, the Netherlands and the United Kingdom the balance of trade in tourism is substantially in the red.[7]

According to OECD figures, passenger transport and travel figure among the biggest service exports within tourism, accounting for more than one third of all international trade in services (i.e. close to 5 per cent of all trade in goods and services in the OECD area) and their growth has outstripped that of services generally.[8] A Commission survey of 1986 revealed that approximately 56 per cent of EC citizens went on holiday at least once in 1985. Twenty per cent of those went abroad to another Member State and 13 per cent elsewhere in Europe or beyond. Fifty-two per cent went to the seaside, 25 per cent into the countryside, 23 per cent into the mountains and 19 per cent into towns. Sixty-eight per cent went by car, 14 per cent by train, 13 per cent by aeroplane, and 5 per cent by boat. For accommodation, 32 per cent stayed in hotels, 21 per cent with relatives or friends, 17 per cent chose to rent, 16 per cent went camping or caravanning, 7 per cent used their holiday homes and 5 per cent stayed in private houses. The holidaymakers' satisfaction indicator, measured on a ten-point scale was as high as 8.17.[9]

TOURISM AND OTHER POLICIES

Tourism improves balance of payments stability between Northern and Southern European countries and it is also seen as a means to assist in the development of the poorest regions in the Community. In more recent years it is increasingly felt, by the Economic and Social Committee, for example, that there is a need for a serious examination of the future of tourism and its contribution to regional development in its widest sense, including town and country planning where relevant. The Economic and Social Committee further wishes to see a more comprehensive policy which underlines the economic and social importance of tourism in the sphere of regional policy and job creation.[10]

Tourism is also important to the Community because of the large number of policies, activities and developments that are directly or indirectly connected with it, such as the free movement of persons, the freedom to provide services, the transport policy, rules on the environment and social development. Most of these policies will be dealt with in some detail later.[11]

Since a number of policies are affected by tourism it is felt that other EC policies and developments must take tourist trends fully into consideration. The link between tourism and the environment is stressed in particular and the Economic and Social Committee has gone as far as to suggest that the European Environmental Agency should include a department specifically concerned with tourism.[12] In its initial guidelines for a Community policy on tourism the European Commission listed as areas in which tourism should be taken into account the following:

- the freedom of movement and the protection of tourists;
- working conditions for those engaged in tourism;
- transport;
- regional development;
- safeguarding of the European heritage.[13]

The Commission's initial attitude was to leave the main responsibilities for tourism to rest on the shoulders of the Member States and it did not wish to go too far in seeking to co-ordinate national policies reflecting the very different situations in the Member States. Rather, it rather wished to pinpoint a number of common priorities in certain spheres on which actions might be proposed. In its opinion on tourism of February 1984 the Economic and Social Committee (ESC), which from an early date has shown profound interest in tourism, did not see any need for reticence in presenting the Council with recommendations over and above those of the guidelines.[14]

Already at that time the Committee recognized that the guidelines could provide a considerable political impetus towards the achievement of a veritable Internal Market and serve as a catalyst for action in fields where progress was blocked. It therefore suggested that Member States, in the preparation and implementation of their national tourism policies, should take into consideration the need to develop an as perfect as possible common tourism market. The Commission also promised in its initial guidelines that it would see to it that national subsidies would conform to the competition rules of the Treaty.

EARLY PLANS AND CHANGES IN TOURISM

With regard to priorities the Commission indicated that it was ready to consider with the Member States *inter alia* the lengthening of the tourist season, the preservation of the architectural heritage in disadvantaged regions and the promotion of social, cultural and rural tourism. In other words, it was interested in tackling the question of how best to use the tourist installations and labour available (especially in rural areas) while encouraging the least privileged in society to become involved in tourism. It was also already envisaging the staggering of holidays to deal with the problem of the saturation of the coastal areas of some countries which cannot solve this problem on their own. holidays must be better staggered in the countries from where the tourists are coming. This evidently requires some degree of co-ordination at European level. The Commission further expressed the wish to play a role in the promotion of tourism and to secure involvment in joint promotional campaigns.

More recently, in the face of competition from outside the EC, the Commission has also been working on joint promotional activity on certain markets outside the EC. A first experiment concerns the USA.[15] Community tourism cannot be taken for granted, despite all the attractions Europe has such as its diversity, high level of development or its heritage and history: competition from other parts of the world such as America and Japan is emerging.

The Commission is not only thinking in terms of holiday related tourism. It employs a much wider concept such as that used by the World Tourism Organisation and the OECD.[16] According to this definition tourism includes all journeys of more than twenty-four hours for recreation, business, study or health purposes. The ESC is of the opinion that the definition should be re-examined and has advocated that for the purposes of the EC a very broad definition should be adopted.[17] For the ESC, tourism is also a human and cultural activity concerned with the quality of life and living standards of the people in general and of those in local communities and neighbourhoods visited by tourists in particular. It is not merely an activity connected with tour operators, travel agents, transport and hotels etc. The social as well as the economic and cultural aspects of Tourism are emphasized by the ESC.[18]

The Commission does not overlook the social side of tourism either: it increasingly pays attention to new forms of tourism such as youth travel, sports travel, travel connected with conferences, etc. Tourism is changing and the Commission is well aware of this. It has pointed out that demographic changes and higher real incomes are bringing about a rise in demand for holidays.[19]

The traditional North–South flow in the EC will change in favour of more travel outside the Community and Western Europe. The increasing number of Southern Europeans taking holidays will also bring changes to which Northern European Countries will have to respond. The spread of technology in the tourist trade in the shape of computerized booking and information systems has also begun to bring major changes to the procedures for holiday travel.

2

Initial Objectives and Themes of Action

For a number of years the Commission's policy has been based on a communication submitted to the Council in January 1986[1] which consists of the following:

- assisting tourism in the EC;
- improving the seasonal and geographical distribution of tourism;
- better use of financial aid;
- better information and protection of tourists;
- improving the working conditions in the tourist industry;
- increasing awareness of the sector, furthering consultation and co-operation.

MEASURES TO FACILITATE TOURISM IN THE COMMUNITY

Obstacles to Citizens and Border Checks.
Intra-Community tourism accounts for most of tourism in the EC (80 per cent). It is therefore obvious that the removal of remaining obstacles to the movement of citizens is of prime importance. The European Parliament has defined the notion of facilitation as 'the means of progressively eliminating all obstacles to the free movement of persons for non-migratory purposes and expanding tourism as a whole'.[2] When the Commission issued its initial guidelines in 1982, twenty-five years after the signature of the EEC Treaty, many border checks were still in existence and even now not all of them have disappeared. However, there has been considerable

progress, particularly during the last few years, as a result of the momentum towards integration created by the Single European Act and the completion of the Internal Market.

Abolition of Checks

Work is underway on a set of measures to allow both nationals of Member States and nationals of third countries to move freely anywhere in the EC.[3] The removal of all checks at internal frontiers was one of the objectives of 1992.

Simplification of Formalities

In 1984 the Council and the Member States adopted a resolution recommending that special checkpoints be set up for the nationals of the Member States and that, wherever possible, frontier formalities be limited to spot checks.[4] Consequently, in July 1984 France and Germany simplified checking procedures (Saarbrücken Agreement) at borders between the two countries.

In 1985 the Commission proposed a Directive to abolish all systematic checks of persons at internal frontiers, whatever the means of transport used.[5] The proposal lays down a number of conditions for easing controls and formalities for individuals at internal frontiers although it does not apply to commercial carriage of goods. Member States will have to ensure that Member States' nationals can cross borders unchecked. Spot checks however, are permitted and so are temporary border controls in special circumstances (e.g. for security purposes). The Directive does not apply to security checks at airports.

Member States' nationals will be permitted to drive across borders at reduced speed (or walk across). A disc bearing the letter E on a green background may be fixed on cars to indicate that all passengers are EC citizens with nothing to declare. Customs signs should be removed from borders and in ports and airports special channels for EC citizens should be set up. There will be no checks on individuals crossing borders on international trains.[6] Some Member States feel that the adoption of this Directive should go together with a resolution on co-operation between the Member States on visa and re-entry policy.

As part of the Schengen Agreement concluded in June 1985, the Benelux Countries, France and Germany adopted the principle of visual checks at road frontiers between the signatory countries with possible spot checks.[7] As seen above, the Commission has similarly proposed that the Member States extend to all land frontiers between them the use of the 'green disc' system which already allows travellers from the Benelux, Germany and France to cross borders between those countries quickly when they have nothing to declare.[8]

The members of the Schengen Group meanwhile will soon be eight since Italy's adoption of an immigration regulation opened the way for its entry into the group on 27 November 1990 in Paris.[9] At the same meeting the member countries granted observer status to Spain and Portugal, as they had done to Italy in 1988. The Schengen Group is playing an important role as a catalyst, 'laboratory' and model for the EC as a whole. Separate channels for EC nationals at airports and borders are already in place in the EC.[10]

Duty Free Goods

As from July 1991 EC citizens may bring back, without any formalities from another Member State, purchases worth 600 ECU (£420). The Council decided on 18 March 1991 to increase the maximum authorized amount from 390 ECU to 600 ECU.[11] This is a record increase. In the past increases in travellers allowances amounted to mere adjustments to offset the effects of inflation on an amount first set in 1969. The present increase really marks a step towards the elimination of formalities for purchases by private individuals in other Member States. As will be seen further on (under tax checks) the twelve also agreed on the principle of border free purchases and purchases without restrictions for private individuals from 1 January 1993. For the time being, the 600 ECU allowance applies only to persons aged 15 years and over; for the under 15-year-olds the allowance is 50 ECU only.

Certain 'sensitive' products will remain subject to quantitative limits: cigarettes (300); wine (5 litres); fortified wine below 22° (3 litres) and spirits over 22° (1.5 litres). In Denmark and Ireland stricter limits were to remain in force until the end of 1991.[12]

Streamlining Complaints Procedure

The Commission feels that consistent efforts to streamline the complaints procedure, including the initiation of infringement procedures, under Articles 30 and 95 EC, should facilitate the removal of obstacles at frontiers and ensure greater tax neutrality.[13] It is also convinced that its intervention in respect of customs disputes (penalties, checks, formalities, procedures), by invoking principles such as the equality principle and the proportionality principle, will continue to make a positive contribution towards the completion of the Internal Market. Such intervention has resulted in a substantial reduction (and in some cases even the reimbursement) of fines which were disproportionate to the offence in question, such as overlooking a detail in the small print of a customs document or failing to present a licence.

Tax Checks

Currently tax checks still exist but the aim is to abolish these as well. The Council adopted a European system of excise duties on 17 December 1990.[14] The aim of this system is to put an end to border checks on alcohol, tobacco products and petrol, while compensating the Member States in which these products are consumed for any loss of tax receipts. From 1 January 1993 such products are not subject to excise duties while they are being transported to another Member State. Private individuals will be able to buy cigarettes, alcoholic beverages and petrol in the country of their choice at prices which are inclusive of all taxes. On May 8 1990 the Commission made a set of proposals for a transitional VAT system for the Single Market and the introduction of a new instrument for administrative co-operation in VAT affairs.[15] This means that private individuals will be able to buy anything anywhere in the EC and pay VAT in the country of purchase. There are some temporary provisions based on the VAT rate of the country of destination, for the sale of cars and mail order sales. For transactions between those subject to the VAT system (companies) a transitional system has been set up which will expire on 13 December 1996. On that day the definitive system of taxation in the Country of origin will apply.

On 3 December 1990 the twelve came to an agreement on VAT.[16] A solution with regard to the actual rates still had to be found. The differences among the twelve are considerable: VAT rates range from a maximum of 12 per cent in Luxembourg to 38 per cent in Italy. Nevertheless these agreements assisted somewhat in meeting the Commission's White Paper objective of the elimination of tax checks following harmonization of rate of VAT and excise duty by 1992. During the Luxembourg Presidency agreement was reached on the level of VAT and excise duty rates to be applied throughout the EC from 1 January 1993 (political agreement for VAT and legally binding agreement on excise duty rates).[17] The agreement was based on Presidency proposals which, contrary to the Commission's proposal, set out minimum rates of VAT and excise duty to apply throughout the EC from 1 January 1993. The Commission's proposals were based on a combination of minimum and maximum rates.[18]

Green Card

Crossings at road frontier posts had already been facilitated in 1972 by the abolition of checks on the international motor vehicle insurance certificate known as the 'green card'.[19] Relevant to tourism is also Commission recommendation 81/76/EEC of 8 January 1981 on accelerated settlement of claims under insurance against civil liability in respect of the use of motor vehicles.[20]

The second Motor Insurance Directive[21] provided further harmonized laws on compulsory motor insurance and, in particular, required the extension of compulsory third party insurance to cover liability for property damage.

During the Irish Presidency a third Directive on Motor liability Insurance was adopted.[22] This increases the level of motor insurance cover required by drivers travelling in Member States with lower compulsory insurance limits.[23] A common position was also agreed in June 1990 with regard to the extension of the scope of the non-life insurance services Directive[24] to include motor liability insurance.

Finally during the Italian Presidency the scope of the non-life insurance services Directive (88/357/EEC) was indeed extended to include motor liability insurance.[25]

Driving Licence

The European driving licence will also facilitate the mobility of tourists. A first step in this direction was made with the First Council Directive[26] which established an EC model national licence, mutual recognition by Member States of national driving licences and the exchange of licences by holders transferring their place of residence or place of employment from one Member State to another.

In January 1989 the Commission presented a proposal for a second Directive on the driving licence replacing Dir. 80/1263/EEC.[27] A standard EC licence has been in existence since 1986 but there are still differences between the Member States in respect of the categories of vehicles, driving tests and minimum age. The Commission wishes to remove these anomalies by laying down guidelines for a Community model licence and to ensure the recognition of a licence issued by one Member State throughout the EC. The obligation to exchange a licence when a person changes residence from one Member State to another is also an obstacle to be removed.

During the Luxembourg Presidency political agreement was reached concerning driving licences.[28] The existing requirement for the compulsory exchange of licences within one year of taking up residence in another Member State will be removed and instead there will be provision for indefinite mutual recognition.

European Passport

The European passport (in force since January 1985) is another example of a measure which can only help to bring about a Europe without frontiers.[29]

The European Parliament is of the view that the European passport confers tangible benefits on the holder and it has invited the Commission to draw up a 'traveller's charter' of EC citizens' rights including: social security provisions, medical and health care rights, rights of establishment, provision of services and for those seeking work, rights to legal aid, access to justice and compensation, and rights regarding duty free purchases and VAT on cross-border transfers of personal possessions.[30]

Transport

It is obvious that additional measures and policies can assist in the elimination of obstacles. The transport policy is a clear example. Greater flexibility in air transport would be helpful; the same goes for better infrastructure in border areas. Railway co-operation, more group tourism, better co-operation with third countries such as Austria and Switzerland could all be beneficial. The Commission is working on all of these and also tries to achieve more rational fixing of fares.[31]

European Card

The Commission is in favour of extending to citizens of all Member States the benefits afforded to certain categories of nationals such as the young, the elderly and the handicapped. The Commission would like to see tourism encouraged among these groups and is thinking of a possible introduction of an easily recognizable 'European card'.[32]

The European Parliament has reiterated its request for the introduction of a 'European young persons travel card'.[33] The Commission has shown concern about road safety while the Economic and Social Committee feels that action in the sphere of tourism will also have to address the problem of health risks which may be spread by EC citizens who return from third countries as well as by non-EC visitors.[34]

Health of Tourists

Currently citizens of the Member States can enjoy benefits under the national medical insurance of other Member States provided they have a sickness insurance form E111, supplied by their own insuring authorities. The administrative formalities involved need simplification since many tourists who have tried to avail themselves of this protection know that the system does not work as well as it should. The Commission wishes to improve the system and keep users better informed. It has been suggested that a more effective arrangement should be introduced which should include the introduction of an internationally recognized document which would entitle the tourist to on-the-spot treatment without any immediate payment, even if he has to make some payment later via administrative channels.[35]

The Council of Ministers has drawn up a model for a European emergency health card containing, in all languages, medical information required for the safety of high risk travellers such as diabetics and people with heart conditions.[36] The ESC has approved the relevant recommendation submitted to the Council by the Commission. Travel is on the increase among some sections of the population including persons suffering from serious or chronic illness (8 to 10 per cent of the population). Such persons may need swift and appropriate medical attention in the event of an accident or illness occurring while they are travelling. Sometimes such persons cannot supply their medical history and often precise information is unavailable. Language problems may make matters even worse.[37] A specimen copy of a European emergency health card can be found in the annex to the Council Resolution on this matter.[38]

Legal Protection

With regard to legal aid problems the Commission would like to see the Member States ratify as soon as possible the 1980 Hague Convention, which gives persons, habitually resident in a contracting state, entitlement to free legal aid for civil and commercial proceedings in other contracting states under the same conditions as nationals of those states.[39] Tourists' legal rights are also protected by the Directive on package holidays which will be dealt with in Chapter 4.[40] The ESC has furthermore asked the Commission what further steps could be taken to help repatriation and compensation of tourists, whether on package tours or not, who find themselves marooned abroad through no fault of their own.[41]

The Free Movement of Capital and Financial Problems

The Treaty of Rome already recognized the free movement of capital as an essential complement to the free movement of goods, people and services. However, progress was not very great in some Member States initially. The United Kingdom abolished all exchange controls in 1979; Germany, France, Italy, Denmark and the Benelux have done the same. The momentum created by the Single European Act no doubt contributed to this process. Other Member States still maintain some controls. A Directive removing controls from all capital movements was adopted in June 1988. The other Member States had until the end of 1992 to comply while Spain and Greece may be given a further extension.[42] The objective is complete liberalization of capital movements in the EC.

A Single Market in which goods, services and persons (including tourist services and tourists) circulate freely can only function properly if the related capital movements are unrestricted. In order to complete the Internal Market restrictions on capital transfers had to be abolished and EC citizens given access to the financial system and products of Member States. Despite some progress in the early years of operation of the EC and the unilateral liberalization by some Member States a great number of restrictions remained in force. In the meantime, however, the three Directives contained in the Commission's White Paper of 1985 have been adopted. The first one is the above-mentioned Directive 88/361/EEC of 24 June 1988, which aimed to remove the remaining restrictions on capital movements between the Member States as part of the completion of the Internal Market and constitutes a major achievement. The deadline for implementing national legislation was 1 July 1990. In order to eliminate or reduce risks of distortion, tax evasion and avoidance linked to the diversity of national systems for taxation of savings and for controlling application of these systems the Commission has presented a follow up proposal.[43]

The second measure, Council Directive 86/566/EEC of 17 November 1986,[44] amending the First Directive of 11 May 1960 on the implementation of Article 67 EEC, liberalizes cross-frontier movements relating to:

- admission of securities to the capital markets;
- transactions in securities not dealt in on the stock exchange;
- long term commercial loans;
- UCITS (for example unit trusts).

The third Council Directive 85/583/EEC of 20 December 1985,[45] amending the Directive of 11 May 1960, has similar provisions purely related to UCITS.[46] Furthermore, in order to fight money-laundering the Commission presented a proposal for a Directive to the Council in March 1990.[47] The aim was to make money-laundering an offence in all Member States and to impose obligations on banks and financial institutions to report suspect financial transactions involving drug trafficking, terrorism and other forms of organized crime. During the Luxembourg Presidency the measure[48] on money-laundering was adopted.

Payments in the Internal Market

The Commission has also issued a discussion document on payments in the Internal Market which points out certain shortcomings in respect of financial transfers between Member States.[49] The Commission would like to see certain improvements, since efficient payment systems are required for the proper operation of any integrated economic system. Currently the national systems are insufficiently interconnected. Transfrontier payments are not only slower but also more expensive and less reliable than purely national ones. The Commission has suggested a structure to interconnect the national clearing houses and the creation of a payments co-ordination group having already issued a recommendation on the transparency of banking conditions relating to cross-border financial transactions.[50]

The Commission is of the opinion that common principles of transparency in respect of the information to be supplied and the details indicated on the statement relating to the transfer of funds would encourage institutions to estimate their costs more accurately and to rationalize their methods of transfer. The situation with regard to bank transfers, cash operations, cheques and payment cards was also reviewed by the Commission's services. The European Parliament asked the Commission to undertake an examination of the role and functions of credit card payments as they apply in the tourist sector, paying attention, in particular, to the level of additional costs which these systems of payment impose on the industry and the consumer.[51] Electronic card payment systems are also of great help in the simplification of payment and withdrawal procedures in all Member States.

Freedom to Receive Services

To pay for services one receives in another Member State one may have to export cash or cheques. The European Court has held, in joint cases 26/83 Luisi v Ministero del Tesoro and 286/82 Carbone v Ministero del Tesoro, that persons travelling for the purpose of tourism, business, education and health are receiving services. Therefore they may not be subject to restrictions in respect of payments. Member States may retain controls only for the purpose of checking the nature of transactions (i.e. to ensure that they are really currency transfers for the purpose of tourism). Luisi and Carbone were criminally prosecuted in Italy for breach of currency regulations. They were accused of taking out of the country foreign currency in excess of the maximum permitted by Italian law. The money had been taken out for the purpose of tourism and medical treatment. The ECJ, on referral, had to deal with the question whether payment for such services constituted movements of capital or payments for the provision of services. The Court found the money to be payment for services and ruled that freedom to provide services included the freedom for recipients of services to go to another Member State to receive a service there.[52]

The Commission feels that exchange controls considered necessary by certain Member States should not form obstacles to tourism. The ECU does not yet exist as a currency in its own right. However, it could be used as the basic comparative unit and contracts be denominated in ECU. ECU travellers' cheques are available in all Member States and there is even a credit card in ECU. The Commission is actively promoting the ECU for these purposes.

Visas

It would be useful if visas for nationals of third countries issued in one Member State were to allow entry to other Member States as well. Currently visas can form obstacles to tourism. The Commission is working on this matter as well as on residence permit systems which also should be integrated to some degree on a community basis. The Commission feels that a common visa valid for all twelve countries, which has been under discussion for some time, should in principle allow a citizen from a third country, after he has been checked at an external frontier, to benefit from the right to move throughout the other Member States without the need of other visas. At Maastricht it was agreed that the Council (according to a Treaty of Rome procedure) will decide by unanimity on the basis of a Commission proposal which third countries require a visa to enter the EC. Qualified majority voting will apply from 1 January 1996. Emergency action can be taken for six months to deal with a sudden crisis and a uniform visa format will be decided.[53] The recent changes in Central and Eastern Europe have already led the twelve Member States to abolish the visa requirement for Hungary, Czechoslovakia[54] and Poland as from 1 July 1992. It is important to consider that entry requirements may constitute obstacles to the development of tourism in some circumstances.

Work is also being done by the Member States on the co-ordination of Member States' policies on terrorism, drug trafficking and co-operation between security forces. At Maastricht it was established that justice and home affairs remain an intergovernmental pillar of the Union Treaty, albeit that the Commission is associated with decision-making and has limited powers of initiative. The areas of common interest include:

- asylum policy;
- rules and controls on persons crossing EC external borders;
- immigration policy;
- combating fraud and drug addiction;
- judicial co-operation in civil and criminal matters;
- customs co-operation;
- police cooperation.

In addition, a Union-wide system for exchanging information between European police forces (Europol) is to be set up.[55]

Freedom of Movement of Tourists in the EC

In the context of this section a few words should be said about the concept of the free movement of persons and what it means for tourists. The EEC Treaty aims to abolish obstacles to the freedom of movement of persons, services and capital. Articles 48, 52 and 59 dealing respectively with workers, the right of establishment and the right to provide services do not refer in any way to persons such as tourists who do not intend to carry out any economic activities while abroad. Therefore tourists *prima facie* do not seem to be covered. However, as can be seen elsewhere in this book, European law has firmly put the tourist on the map:

(a) through the effect of the Single European Act and the completion of the Single Market, as will be explained in Chapter 3;
(b) by above-mentioned rulings by the European Court concerning Mrs Luisi and Mr Carbone, in which it was held that Articles 59 and 60 EEC also cover the recipients of services.[56]

In the Court's view tourists must be considered as recipients of services and payments concerning the receipt of such services abroad should not be restricted under Article 106 (1). In other words, tourists come squarely within the Treaty's scope. The European Court has even gone so far as to rule that tourist recipients of services have the right to compensation in assault cases.[57] Mr Cowan, a British citizen who was visiting his son in Paris and who had been the victim of an assault at the exit from a Metro station, successfully relied on Article 7 EEC. The ECJ held that in the case of persons to whom EC law guaranteed the freedom to travel to another Member State, in particular as a recipient of services, the principle of nondiscriminatrion laid down in Article 7 EEC prevented that state from making the grant of state compensation for physical injury caused to the victim of an assault in that state subject to the condition either that he held a residence permit or that he was a national of a country which had a reciprocal agreement with that Member State. The Court recalled that although criminal legislation and criminal procedural rules fell in principle within the competence of Member States, it was well established that EC law defined the limits to that competence. The same approach, as in the Luisi and Carbone rulings, is taken in EC legislation.[58]

Member States must abolish restrictions on the movement and residence of nationals of Member States who wish to go to another Member State as recipients of services. It has been pointed out that tourists can be recipients of services, irrespective of the existence of a pre-established service transaction. But it could also be argued that when crossing a frontier in order to receive services, an individual should have the necessary financial means to do so:[59] Van der Woude and Mead disagree.[60] One must agree that since the free movement of workers with all the possible negative financial consequences for the host Member State is allowed under the EEC Treaty, it seems contradictory to restrict tourism especially as tourism generates additional revenue. Such qualification would also be incompatible with the concept of a People's Europe. It goes without saying that a tourist by definition must return to his normal place of residence. The abolition of internal controls is closely linked with the unification of external controls; the gradual decrease of internal checks must be accompanied by a gradual increase in external checks.

An intergovernmental convention aimed at laying down rules on the crossing of the Community's external borders has run into some difficulties over the inclusion of ports and airports.[61] Most Member States and the Commission favour a solution which contributes to an area without internal frontiers regardless of the mode of transport used and irrespective of the nationality of the traveller. Work is also being undertaken on police co-operation which will be needed after abolition of internal controls.

DISTRIBUTION OF TOURISM

As many as 62 per cent of EC holidaymakers take their holiday in July and August.[62] Such concentration leads to all sorts of unacceptable consequences such as congestion, less road safety, higher holiday prices. It causes not only overwork but also unemployment. The transport infrastructure, accomodation and other facilities are saturated during the high season and underused during other parts of the year. The quality of the environment also suffers and there are negative consequences for regional development. The problem exists in all Member States and in those visited or passed through by great numbers of tourists in particular. The Commission, in its communication to the Council of 1986, recommended that special attention should be paid to the environment in this respect.[63] Ironically, there is insufficient awareness of the fact that beaches, mountains, wildlife, countryside, historic towns, monuments and sites are the basic resources on which tourism depends. Neither is there sufficient planning and application at government level with the result that the environment has already seriously deteriorated. The Commission has furthermore pointed out that the tourist industry, even if it makes its profits from these resources, is not involved in their conservation. Therefore the EC aims to integrate conservation of the environment in the planning and development of tourism. As was pointed out above, staggering of holidays is one way to bring about and maintain a more balanced policy. Proper marketing of resources is another way in which saturation of heavily visited areas could be relieved. Progress in the sphere of environmental legislation is also relevant: for example, under the Directive on evaluation of the of the effects of certain public and private projects on the environment, some tourist projects could be examined in an early stage.[64]

Progress with regard to staggering of holidays will be made only slowly. Apart from obstacles such as the existing system of holidays there are old habits and attitudes which will not change overnight. For the Commission the staggering of holidays is nevertheless of prime importance. It is also important that when they are introducing measures to stagger holidays Member States do so in collaboration with one another and in co-ordination with the Commission, which is ready to support their efforts in close co-operation with other international organizations such as the Council of Europe and the World Tourism Organization. The Commission prepared a proposal for a Council resolution on a better seasonal and geographical distribution of tourism which was adopted by the Council on 22 December 1986.[65] It was invited by the Council Resolution of 10 April 1984 on a Community policy on tourism[66] to present proposals, notably with a view to facilitating Tourism within the Community.

The proposal on seasonal and geographical distribution has to be seen in this context. The Commission had pointed out that in order to avoid and resolve saturation problems in tourist and transit areas there is a need to measure capacity, to assess the risks of saturation and to take measures particularly in respect of the environment. The seasonal nature of tourist activities causes problems for local population and tourist alike during the short holiday periods and facilities are underused during the rest of the year. Therefore the Member States were invited to measure the capacity of tourist areas and to assess the risks and effects of saturation during certain periods of the year, in particular by means of impact studies. Member States were also invited to stop providing incentives to development in saturated areas and to prohibit or at least discourage further construction in such areas. They should encourage measures reducing the causes of overload and develop facilities in areas and sites where the risk of saturation is low. National tourist boards and other competent authorities should do less to promote saturated areas and more to promote those with surplus capacity. They are also asked to do more to promote alternative types of holidays and holidays out of season, with respect to environmental needs.

The Commission is playing a central role in the search for solutions through co-ordination, studies, exchange of information and other appropriate measures. For example the Commission has supported a Dutch initiative relating to the organization of a conference on the staggering of holidays, which took place meanwhile at Noordwijk in the Netherlands, on 16 and 17 October 1991, during the Dutch Presidency. The Conference was organized by the Netherlands Ministry of Economic affairs. More than 120 delegates from twenty-two countries participated. One of the conclusions was that a successful approach for improving the seasonal spread demands co-operation between the private and public sectors, at regional, national and international level. The international dimension of the seasonal spread, although it becomes more and more important, has hardly been recognized until now. The conference furthermore identified a need for an organizational framework for exchange of information and co-operation between the public and private sectors. It defined a number of recommendations, aimed at the international governmental level, the national and regional governmental level and at the level of the industry itself.[67] In order to improve knowledge of the tourist industry the Commission has undertaken a study entitled 'The experience, products and suitable clientèle for all season tourism'.[68] The Commission indeed plays a major role in encouraging and co-ordinating national and regional measures and initiatives to improve the staggering of holidays in the EC.

It has been pointed out by the Economic and Social Committee that the time is ripe to move from the phase of merely searching for solutions to taking positive action drawing on research work already done including that undertaken by outside specialists.[69] The Committee more generally does not believe that the lack of reliable information on tourism in the EC is an impediment to effecting a serious assessment of its present situation or development. It does, however, warn against conducting research for its own sake and points out that the amount of research already carried out by international bodies such as the European Travel Commission, the OECD and the World Tourism Organisation, as well as work subcontracted to outside specialists by the Commission itself, should be sufficient for the Commission to formulate more proposals on tourism.

With regard to distribution of tourism, the Commission is looking closely at three types – social, rural and cultural tourism.[70] Social tourism would benefit the less privileged; cultural tourism can more easily be 'deseasonalized' since it is relatively independent of weather conditions. The Commission is also studying ways of promoting holiday-making on farms or in rural areas, such as support for the training of operators and aid for improving the rural habitat. Each of these types serves the preferences, tastes and interests of particular categories of tourists and it is hoped that they will assist in improving both the seasonal and geographical distribution of tourism.

Social Tourism

Social tourism is tourism organized by nonprofit-making associations (such as friendly societies, co-operatives and trade unions) with the objective of making tourism available to the less well off in society. (One is thinking in particular of families, young people, the handicapped and pensioners.) This form of tourism was introduced in several industrialized countries of Europe after the right to paid holidays was acquired. According to the Commission, in the countries where it already exists (such as Belgium, Denmark, France and Italy) social tourism has had a beneficial effect on regional development and the employment situation in areas previously without commercial tourism (notably in mountain and rural areas and hinterlands). Two types of aids which have to be compatible with Articles 92 and 93 of the EEC Treaty are relevant to the concept of social tourism.

First of all there is aid to buildings (mainly in Belgium, Denmark and France). This subsidy is provided in various forms by public or semi-public authorities, to facilitate the construction of tourist facilities managed by co-operatives or other nonprofit-making organizations. Apart from aid to buildings there is aid to people (France and Greece) which consists of holiday bonuses, holiday vouchers granted on the basis of family income and situation by works committees and certain welfare institutions (pension funds) and holiday cheques paid for by worker contributions and subsidies from employers.[71] As a result of such aids not only a greater number of EC citizens can indeed go on holiday but also the objective of a seasonal and geographical distribution will be met more effectively. The Commission feels that such facilities must also be publicized among and be available to the social categories in question, such as large families, young people and pensioners in all Member States. Travel assistance should be available throughout the EC and reductions (for travel, entrance to museums and access to leisure facilities etc.) should exist for nationals and citizens of other Member States alike. The Commission has also advocated a guide to social tourism in the EC.

There are other ways to encourage social tourism to be considered, such as joint projects by several Member States, part-financed by existing Community funds or under the integrated Mediterranean programmes[72] and measures to encourage exchanges of young people and vocational training for those employed in the tourist industry, particularly in social tourism.[73] The Economic and Social Committee, in its report on Tourism and Regional Development of 1990, has stressed that the EC as well as national and local authorities should support schemes to promote social tourism, including all forms of exchange schemes such as town twinning. It further feels that it is important that social tourism be integrated with the local economy, for example the network of tourist villages (Eurovillages) proposed by the International Office for Social Tourism (BITS). Villages Vacances Familles (VVF) is the leading European organization engaged in the provision of subsidized holiday facilities. The establishment of Eurovillages which are an extension at European level of the VVF formula has made the association prominent among other associations providing subsidized facilities in Europe.[74] The ESC has even called for EC finance for a study of the means of setting up a European Community social tourism operator whose main aim would be the development of low season holidays for the elderly and the young.

Rural Tourism

Apart from social and cultural tourism the Commission is also studying ways of promoting holiday-making on farms or in rural areas, such as support for the training of operators and aid for improving the rural habitat. Meanwhile, it has adopted a Community action to promote such forms of tourism.[75] In the Commission's view, rural tourism is a broad concept, covering more than mere farm tourism or agritourism (i.e. accomodation provided by farmers). It concerns all tourist activities in rural areas. The Economic and Social Committee has asked the Commission to define rural and agritourism more precisely in order to bring these terms into line with national laws and regulations. Since rural tourism (as cultural tourism) is less dependent on weather conditions than mass tourism it is obvious that rural tourism also could contribute to a better seasonal and geographical distribution of tourism. The Commission has also advocated the standardization of information on accommodation in rural areas along the lines of that of hotels (see further Chapters 4 and 5). It is also prepared to consider other ways of encouraging this form of tourism with national experts, such as better publicity for traditional cultural events in rural areas; the feasibility of restoring, improving and re-utilizing the rural habitat for tourist purposes, a feasibility study on the introduction of standardized road signs to indicate accommodation in rural areas; and the use of posters to advertise rural tourism at agricultural and tourist fairs.[76]

In this field too, as in the area of social tourism, the Commission has advocated the compilation of a guide. The measures to be taken to assist rural tourism business include help to define, create and develop rural tourism products as well as the promotion of access to the market in rural tourism. This development presents opportunities for tourism business in rural areas, but they should anticipate that they will have to satisfy a more demanding and articulate customer who can afford to pick and choose. However, the EC can provide assistance: several measures are already available to the rural tourism business, in particular under the CAP.[77] Assistance is also provided under the ERDF (European Regional Development Fund). As part of European Tourism year (EYT) (See Chapter 3) the Commission has strengthened its links with a multitude of national and European Tourism organizations.

Assistance for rural tourism is further available under schemes such as the Community rural development initiative LEADER (Links between actions for the development of the rural economy) under which the EC will ecourage integrated rural development at local level.[78] The EC also aims to promote integration of rural tourism into promotional and sales systems such as tourist offices, tour operators and travel agencies.

Cultural Tourism

Cultural tourism is of great importance to the Community. Not only is it one of the easiest types of tourism to be 'deseasonalized' but it also confronts Europeans with the reality of their shared inheritance. In other words, it aids European integration. Furthermore, it is of great significance economically since traditionally it has drawn tourists from third countries to Europe with its rich cultural and architectural heritage. There is great scope for further development in this respect. The objective of cultural tourism is to improve general knowledge of history, art and social customs. Seasonal distribution can be realized in particular if tourist areas can offer high levels of cultural activity such as museums, concerts, exhibitions, folklore, etc. in the low season.

The Commission is available to co-operate with national bodies and with the Council of Europe to encourage joint action on specific themes and expressions of European culture.[79] For example, the Commission has been involved in pilot projects for European cultural itineraries, advantageously priced and aimed at certain categories of citizens such as young people, pensioners and research workers (see also Chapter 3 and 5). The Commission would also like to see more resources available to preserve and restore our architectural heritage. Some aid has already come forward from the EC budget and there has been assistance from the European Investment Bank, which has put up funds on several occasions towards protecting or making the most of historic sites and monuments of importance for Europe's cultural heritage.[80] An example of such a scheme in Greece is the museum on the island of Milos in the Cyclades safeguarding works of art and archaeological findings of the finest quality and also providing a major tourist attraction on an island where tourism is of crucial importance to the economy. Examples in Italy are the restoration the Doge's Palace in Venice and development and protection of the archaeological sites in Herculaneum, Pompeii and Stabiae.

The Commission feels that the European Historic Monuments and Sites Fund, which already undertakes worthwhile projects but on too limited a scale, must be expanded if its contribution is to be effective. The Economic and Social Committee has stressed that cultural tourism should not be concerned only with the artistic and cultural heritage of a region but also with its contemporary creativity.[81] It is perhaps true that those who visit a region for mainly cultural purposes (monuments, museums, theatres, art galleries, etc.) are as a rule more inclined to seek contact with the local population and to show greater tolerance and understanding of local characteristics and customs. It is even suggested that such tourists are more considerate in respect of the environment and are more likely to set a good example and to provide the local population with a greater sense of worth of their surroundings. It is also undeniable that cultural tourism stimulates creativity, and indeed many artists, thinkers and people of action have gained creative inspiration from cultural travel. Cultural tourism has great advantages, attractions and potential. It could mean enhanced enjoyment because of less crowded destinations, greater revenue for the businesses involved and at the same time less expense for those taking advantage of trips in the low season.

The Economic and Social Committee has called for comprehensive action to meet the needs of all-year-round visits to monuments and museums, such as increased publicity, upgrading of the image of cultural tourism, incentives to tour operators and the protection of cultural sites from looting.[82] The EC, national governments as well as local authorities, should pay particular attention to:

- the protection, promotion and full use of historic and cultural sites and monuments as well as natural beauty spots;
- the organization and marketing of cultural events and recreational programmes;
- the promotion in third countries of the image of Europe as a cultural destination both in ancient and modern terms.

BETTER USE OF FINANCIAL AID

At present the EC contributes to various tourism projects through financial instruments such as the ERDF, the Social Fund, the EAGGF, the NCI and the IMPs. In the context of the latter, the IMPs (Integrated Mediterranean Programmes) the EC may finance not only the building and modernization of hotels, rural accommodation and other installations and infrastructure related to tourism development, but also promotional publicity and touristic animation activities.

The EAGGF is already in a position to assist in the geographical distribution of tourism. Unfortunately the Member States do not yet make full use of its facilities. The Commission aims to make better use of existing financial instruments to aid tourism, particularly, as pointed out above, to improve its distribution.[83] The Commission is aware of the importance of establishing an adequate coherence between the development of tourism and other regional development. It has moreover promised a special brochure to provide better information on the availability of EC funds for tourists, for both public and private organizations active in this field. The ESC feels, in respect of the EC's financial instruments, that there should be more concrete proposals and it has reiterated what it said in its opinion of 1983, – that the Commission should have a budget for promoting an EC policy on tourism.[84] The ESC furthermore complained that the EIB (the EC's key financial instrument) was not even listed as one of the instruments that might assist tourism and should therefore be included.

EIB Support

It would be wrong to think, however that the EIB has not been instrumental in the expansion of tourist activity since over the years the European Bank has been mounting an increasing number of operations in support of tourism, provided that the schemes in question complied with the economic policy objectives of the EEC Treaty, most notably regional development.[85]

Many infrastructure projects attracting EIB support clearly make a direct contribution to the development of tourism.[86] For instance, the major trunk roads and motorways not only carry a great volume of freight traffic but also have to cope with the summer holiday rush. Good examples are the Basque coast motorway, the Brenner motorway, the Autostrada dei Fiori, the Esterel Côte d'Azur motorway and the Fréjus tunnel. Other infrastructure projects supported by the EIB that contribute towards the development of tourism are the bypasses (of Bordeaux, Toulouse, Naples, Palermo, Thionville, Lyon) on the main holiday routes across Europe. Tourism has also benefited from various transport projects supported by the EIB such as ferries on the routes to Ireland, harbour works at Boulogne, Calais and Ramsgate, airport schemes, particularly in Greece, and the acquisition of aircraft to improve links within the EC and serve holiday destinations. One can also think of high speed train services, local road networks in tourist areas in several Member States including the United Kingdom, water schemes to increase supplies in tourist areas, and development of telecommunications. The Bank has also been instrumental in helping to fight pollution and prevent deterioration of resorts, thereby boosting tourism in the Mediterranean and further north in declining industrial areas and those with a high population such as the United Kingdom (Firth of Forth, Wales) where water pollution causes problems for tourism. The EIB has also contributed more directly to developing tourism: it has provided funds to be channelled directly into hotel developments, holiday villages, theme parks, ski-lift equipment and the construction of marinas. It makes finance available for new schemes as well as extensions and rehabilitation work. But it should be said that most operations have been on a rather small scale, mounted via global loans. These are lines of credit advanced generally to banks or financial institutions, on the whole, those operating nationwide although some have a specific regional or sectoral bias. Projects are selected by the intermediary institution with the EIB's agreement and in accordance with the Bank's appraisal criteria.[87] Examples of individual projects financed are the restructuring and modernization of hotels in the least developed regions of the Mezzogiorno, at Avellino, Caserta, Catania, Palermo and Syracuse. At Metaponto support has been given for the construction of a holiday village. Most investments were located in assisted areas. Non assisted areas have benefited from the use of global loan finance from the second tranche of the New Community Instrument for borrowing and lending (NCI), for Tourism projects (mainly in the hotel trade) in France, Italy and the United Kingdom.

The guidelines concerning the third NCI tranche now preclude the deployment of such resources for hotel projects.[88] The European Parliament has commended the EIB for its global loan scheme which can be very beneficial to SME's in the tourist sector, but it has called on it to investigate the possibility of its taking a more active role in promoting investment in the tourism sector instead of relying only on intermediaries.[89] The Parliament also believes that employment and investment in the tourist industry would rise more rapidly if interest rates on EIB loans for tourism related projects were reduced through the use of ERDF grants and if the recipients of such soft loans for small projects were encouraged to participate in management training schemes.

Suggestions for Improvement

The ESC has complained that most of the money invested in the tourist industry, as can be seen for example from the EIB's involvement in this sphere, is spent on infrastructure work, the modernization of existing facilities and training programmes, and only a very small proportion is spent on tourist businesses.[90] The Committee feels therefore that the EC's financial instruments must be strengthened in order to be able to support the EC's policy on tourism and to promote growth in the tourist industry. It furthermore asked for procedures for consultation with the main trade organizations in this sector before any funds are distributed, in order to prevent distortions of competition or squandering of resources. More recently it concluded that the Structural Funds should only be made available for assistance when there is evidence of a framework plan, widely discussed between all responsible authorities, entrepreneurs and social partners, in which the participants are prepared to make a substantial commitment.[91] On the whole there should be no support for isolated projects or piecemeal development.

One must agree with the ECS's complaint that the tourism sector has not yet received adequate financial support. Neither is there a comprehensive programme to promote tourism in the EC and to attract visitors from third countries. However, matters are improving and the EC is stepping up its promotion activities in respect of visitors from outside the Community (see Chapter 5, p. 100). The Commission in its recent action plan to assist tourism seems to agree.[92] It is also aware that better targeting of financial aid is crucial to initiatives in the tourism sector. Specific allocations to tourism from the ERDF increased from less than 1 per cent to more than 3 per cent. There is further improvement with the 1988 reform of the structural funds, enabling tourism to figure as a priority in certain Community Support frameworks (e.g. Greece and Spain) which cover interventions from all structural funds and not merely the ERDF.[93]

The accent in these CSF's is placed on above-mentioned alternative tourism, including cultural tourism, a better distribution of tourism, environmental protection, the provision of basic amenities (such as water) to promote tourism, help to reconversion and development of small hotels, vocational training and support for intermediate services (such as management advice for small firms). As pointed out above in relation to the EIB, much public funding (such as transport infrastructure) does not figure as direct support to tourism, but is evidently of great relevance.

The draft 1989 EC budget set aside EC 1.750.000 for tourism. The ESC has pointed out that this would not even meet the basic financial requirements of the activities in connection with the European Tourism Year and the five-year programme for tourism. The Committee therefore felt that the Parliament rightly increased the appropriation for tourism to 4 million ECU. One can only agree with the ESC when it expressed the view that this is still insufficient for a satisfactory policy for a rational development of tourism. The European Parliament is not satisfied either since it feels that the intervention of the European Regional Fund has so far been circumstantial and not based on an integrated sectoral perspective.[94] It has been principally directed to infrastructure rather than the creation of productive economic activities and is, therefore, not contributing as fully to endogenous regional development as it should.

BETTER INFORMATION AND PROTECTION OF TOURISTS

If there is to be a true Common Market for tourism, travellers need to be better informed about the areas to be visited and available accommodation. The Commission is aware of this and has distributed in co-operation with private bodies a brochure entitled *Travelling in Europe*.[95] The brochure contains useful information on subjects such as the crossing of borders, duty-free allowances and health care. The Commission, however, feels that a much more complete guide is required, giving more practical information on all Member States (including matters such as opening times of museums, services and main holidays). Such a brochure is seen as part and parcel of the work on a People's Europe.

With regard to information on hotels it would be ideal to have a complete classification of hotels covering all Member States. This appears difficult to achieve. However the Council has approved a recommendation drafted by the Commission in consultation with the hotel and restaurant industry for standardization of the main information about hotels.[96] The Commission has come to the conclusion that because of differences in climate and customs in the Member States a 'star' type classification system for the entire EC would be difficult to effect but it feels that a standard information system (SIS) is objective, practical and easy to administer and that it will assist the traveller in judging value for money offered by a particular type of accommodation and that it could be adapted for input into a computerized reservation system.[97] (Standardized hotel information will be discussed further in Chapter 4.) The Commission is of the opinion that prices could also be expressed in ECU and that common symbols should be adopted for various facilities offered and it has plans to establish a similar system for camp sites and for social and rural tourism. Such information would be given in the official national guides.[98] The Commission would also like to see all hotel guides in the EC contain an introduction explaining how to use the guide both in the language of the country in question and two further languages. It has suggested the main information to be included in the guide, including opening period, prices, discounts and standardized symbols for various facilities.[99]

With regard to fire safety in hotels there is a Council recommendation of 22 December 1986 on which the Commission urges the

Member States to act.[100] Since some of the Member States had no specific rules in this area this measure, even if it is only soft law, is of great significance for tourism. (The recommendation will be discussed further in Chapter 4.) Considerable progress has also been made with regard to package travel. Tourists using this type of holiday, which involves the supply of services such as travel, accommodation, meals and ancillary services, often complain because of inaccurate information or failure to respect the terms of the contract. For example, according to a survey carried out for the Commission, depending on the country, between 25 and 35 per cent of those who took a foreign holiday using this formula in 1982 and 1983 were dissatisfied.[101] A directive on package travel laying down common rules on package travel and establishing a minimum level of consumer protection was adopted during the Irish Presidency.[102] This measure is crucial to the EC's activities in the sphere of tourism and is of great importance to both consumers and the travel trade and will therefore be discussed in greater detail further on (see Chapter 4 which deals with some actions of major importance). The measure aims to ensure that EC citizens are protected against misinformation concerning package travel, and attempts to define the responsibilities of travel agents and tour operators towards travellers. It also requires organizers and/or retailers to make prompt efforts to find appropriate solutions in cases of complaints and it aims to ensure equal conditions of competition in the package travel sector.

The European Parliament has called on the Member States to make information on special traffic regulations and penalties in all Member States available at all railway stations, airports, ports, travel agencies and tourist information offices.[103] This will prove useful to the tourist since currently there is a great lack of information in this respect both before departure and after arrival at holiday destinations.

THE IMPROVEMENT OF WORKING CONDITIONS, INCLUDING THE RIGHT OF ESTABLISHMENT AND THE FREEDOM TO PROVIDE SERVICES

As pointed out above, the tourist industry is characterized by a heavy concentration of tourists in certain places for a short period and under-utilization of both facilities and manpower during the rest of the year. One of the best ways of remedying this problem, as has been suggested, is to bring about a better seasonal and geographical distribution of tourism. However, more is required, such as a better knowledge of the employment situation. Seasonality has another drawback in that it makes the monitoring of employment difficult. It is also difficult to determine the number of jobs directly dependent on tourism because it is not easy to distinguish between services offered to travellers and those offered to residents, for example in the sphere of transport and restaurants. The Commission wishes to clarify this situation[104] and supports initiatives such as a study of the hotel, restaurant and café subsectors. The introduction of information technology in the travel and tourism industry will obviously enable airlines, railways, travel agencies and hotels to improve and accelerate reservations and confirmations. A study financed by the Commission will facilitate the standardization of computer vocabularies and access to databanks of all Member States.[105]

Vocational Training

With regard to the improvement of vocational training some help can be obtained from the European Social Fund. For example, the Social Fund finances vocational training and retraining for people employed in the tourist industry in sectors such as hotels, restaurants and winter sports.[106] The Fund can also assist projects for the training of craftsmen who produce souvenirs for the tourist industry. In addition the Commission wishes to encourage co-operation not only between educational establishments concerned with tourism, but also between these institutions and the tourist industry, in view of the organization of periods of training abroad for students learning the tourist trade.[107] Training periods abroad are of great importance to such students, particularly from the point of view of language learning and practice.

As far as vocational training for skilled workers is concerned, the Commission has introduced comparability at EC level for eight occupations: receptionist, porter, salesman, domestic help, restaurant, barman, cook and wine waiter.[108]

Tourist Guides

There are also a number of problems specific to certain jobs such as tourist guides when working abroad, because in some Member States the profession is regulated while this is not the case in others.[109] To be more precise there is the possibility of confusion between the activities of tourist guides and those of mere couriers. There are two types of tourist guides. Under the first category come those who accompany tourists to the host Member State, while remaining based in their state of origin; their situation is covered by Article 59 EEC as recently decided by the Court of Justice. Second, there are tourist guides who wish to become established in another Member State; their activities are covered by Article 57 EEC.[110]

The European Court recently ruled that France, Italy and Greece had failed to fulfil their obligations under Article 59 EEC (freedom to provide services) by requiring tourist guides accompanying a group of tourists from another Member State to hold a licence.[111] Although the Court accepted that the public interest and the objective of consumer protection could constitute an imperative reason for the justification of a restriction of the freedom to provide services, the requirements in question went beyond what was necessary. The effect of the licence requirement was to reduce the number of guides who accompanied tourists. Tour operators might give preference to local guides. Tourists might end up with guides who were not familiar with their language, their interest and specific wishes. The Court further pointed out that, since travel operators had to maintain their reputation, the pressure of competition leads to guides being selected to a certain degree and provided a check on the quality of their services.

The European Court already held in case 168/85 that the Italian Republic failed to fulfil its obligations under Articles 48, 52 and 59 EEC by maintaining in force provisions which made reciprocity a condition for the treatment of foreign nationals in the same manner as Italian nationals in regard to certain occupations in the field of tourism.[112] In this judgement the Court took the same attitude to the maintaining in force of provisions which made Italian nationality a condition for registration as a trainee journalist or as a regular contributor to publications and made reciprocity a condition for the inclusion of professional journalists who are nationals of other Member States on the special register of foreign journalists. Italy had furthermore failed to fulfil its obligations under the Treaty by maintaining in force provisions permitting only Italian nationals to take part in competitions for the award of licences to operate pharmacies. The Court did not accept the Italian Government's argument, that in view of the direct applicability of above-mentioned provisions of the Treaty, the rights of nationals of other Member States were sufficiently guaranteed by circulars or administrative Directives. Such an argument could not be pleaded in defence of the Commission's complaint with regard to the access to the various activities in the field of tourism. The Italian government had not shown that it had issued any circular or administrative Directive in relation to the access of nationals of other Member States to such activities. Simple administrative practices which by their nature could be altered as it pleased the administration and were not given sufficient publicity could not be regarded as constituting proper implementation of the obligations of the Treaty.

In a case involving tourism and the right of residence and establishment, the European Court recently had to deal with a request for a preliminary ruling from the Tribunal Administratif Papeete (Polynesia).[113] The question was raised in two cases concerning decisions in which the High Commissioner of the French Republic in Polynesia refused to grant a residence permit to Peter Kaefer, a German tourist, and ordered the expulsion from that territory of Andrea Procacci, who held a Swiss passport but claimed to be of Italian nationality. Both applied for annulment of the decisions against them maintaining that they had been adopted contrary to Council Decision 86/283/EEC of 30 June 1986. The Court held that the sphere of application of Article 176 of Council Decision 86/283/EEC on the association of overseas countries and territories with the EC does not extend to cover decisions taken by the competent authorities of the Member States with regard to entry and residence of nationals of the other Member States in an overseas territory, except where such decisions concern the nationals of the other Member States who exercise or seek to exercise the right of establishment or the freedom to provide services in such a territory.

The prohibition of discrimination laid down by Article 176 of above-mentioned Council Decision may be relied on before the competent authorities of a country or a territory by a national of a Member State, other than the one with which that country or territory maintains special relations, for the purpose of establishing himself or providing services there, once the person concerned satisfies the conditions required of nationals not established in that country or territory and if the Member State of which he is a national extends the same treatment to persons from the country or territory in question.

Right of Establishment and the Freedom to Provide Services

Several Directives on the right of establishment and the freedom to supply services, and certain transitional measures, apply to the tourist industry – restaurants, cafés, hotels and camping sites, couriers and travel agents.[114] One of these is Council Directive 68/367/EEC of 15 October 1968 on transitional measures in respect of activities of self-employed persons in the personal services sector (ex ISIC Division 85): 1 – Restaurants, cafés, taverns and other drinking and eating places (ISIC Group 852) 2 – Hotels, rooming houses, camps and other lodging places (ISIC Group 853).[115] Another one is Council Directive 75/368/EEC of 16 June 1975 on measures to facilitate the effective exercise of freedom of establishment and freeedom to provide services in respect of various activities (ex ISIC Divisions 01 to 85) and in particular, transitional measures in respect of those activities.[116]

Note that the latter directive of 16 June 1975 includes within its scope couriers and interpreter guides. Another relevant measure is the Directive on measures to encourage the right to freedom of establishment and freedom to provide services by self-employed workers, including certain transport auxiliaries and travel agents.[117] Important for self-employed persons is also Regulation No 1390/81 of May 1981, which extends Regulation No 1408/71 on the application of social security schemes to self-employed persons and their families .[118]

Recognition of Qualifications

An important Council Directive of 21 December 1988 introduced a general system for the recognition of higher education diplomas awarded on completion of professional education and training of at least a three year duration.[119] This Directive has been in force since January 1991 and is applicable to all professions which require at least three years training at university level or equivalent. A similar Directive is in the pipeline on a system for the mutual recognition of vocational training provided at secondary education level or in the form of short higher education courses and experience rather than a qualification for certain occupations.[120]

The logic of the Internal Market is that individuals should be in a position to exercise their occupation anywhere in the EC and that they should not be hindered by national legislation. The new Directive will not replace the more specific ones already in existence or the transitional measures, particularly those relating to tourist occupations, where these have already introduced mutual recognition. To that extent the transitional measures would become permanent. Directive 75/368/EEC[121] on transitional measures directly regulates the freedom of establishment of tour operators in the sense of persons organizing package holidays and persons accompanying tourists, but not persons who give detailed explanations of sites, etc.[122]

Personal Services Sector

Above-mentioned Directive 68/367 applies to activities in the personal services sector (ISIC Major Group 85), i.e. restaurants, cafés, taverns and other drinking and eating places (ISIC Group 852) and motels, rooming houses, camps and other lodging places (ISIC Group 853). According to Article 2(2) the term 'activities falling within Group 852' refers to activities pursued by a natural person, or company or firm, who habitually and by way of trade and in his own name and on his own account serves prepared food or beverages for consumption on the premises in the establishment or establishments run by him. The serving of meals for consumption elsewhere than on the premises where they are prepared is also covered. It is not applicable to the serving of prepared food or beverages intended for immediate comsumption if such serving is done by way of itinerant trade.

'Activities falling within Group 853' thus mean activities pursued by a natural person, or company or firm, who habitually and by way of trade supplies in his own name and on his own account:

- furnished lodgings or furnished rooms in an establishment or establishments run by him;
- camping facilities on specially equipped sites, designed for short-term stays;
- the services, in each case, normally associated therewith

Apart from restrictions a number of other measures and discriminatory laws listed in Article 3 had to be abolished. For example the

French rule preventing foreign nationals pursuing the occupation of retailer of alcoholic beverages for consumption on the premises or the Italian rule that only Italians may pursue the occupation of manager of mountain refuge stations.[123]

Directive 68/368[124] lays down provisions on transitional measures relating to activities of self-employed persons (ISIC Major Group 85) in the personal services sector, i.e. restaurants, cafés, taverns and other drinking and eating places (ISIC Group 852) and hotels, boarding houses, camps and other lodging places (ISIC Group 853). In respect of activity which depends upon the possession of general, commercial or professional knowledge the host state shall be satisfied where such activity has been pursued in another Member State during the following periods:

- three consecutive years in an independent or managerial capacity;
- two consecutive years in such capacity where there is proof of previous training;
- two consecutive years in such capacity where there is proof that the activity has been pursued for at least three years in a non-independent capacity;
- four consecutive years in a non-independent capacity, where the beneficiary can prove that he has received previous training.

If it so requires of its own nationals, the host country may, furthermore, demand that the activity in question should have been pursued, and vocational training received, in the branch of trade in the host country in which the beneficiary wishes to establish himself. Member States' certificates for the pursuit of activities envisaged under Directive 68/368 ideally should conform to the model set out in the annex.[125]

Various Activities

Above-mentioned Directive 75/368, in order to fill certain gaps, provides measures to facilitate the effective exercise of freedom of establishment and freedom to supply services together with transitional measures relating to a very wide range of activities (ex ISIC Division OI to 85).[126] It excludes activities such as transport, itinerant trade and those involving the use of toxic products regulated by the relevant directives. It furthermore excludes the activities of tourist guides except those of couriers and interpreter-guides listed in the annex.

The Directive distinguishes between activities that do require a period of extensive professional training and those that do not. In the first case there tend to be stringent national rules. The Directive says in this respect that where the Member State insists upon the possession of general, commercial or professional knowledge and ability for taking up and pursuing an activity, it will accept as sufficient evidence of such requirements the fact that the activity has been pursued elsewhere in the EC for any of the periods laid down in the Directive. Among the many activities included in the list are also community services such as museums, botanical and zoological gardens, recreation services including sporting activities (except the activities of sports instructors) games including racing stables and race-courses; other recreational activities such as circuses, amusement parks and entertainments; personal services not elsewhere classified (with some exceptions such as sports and mountain guides) and many others.

Travel Agencies

As pointed out above, Council Directive 82/470 of 29 June 1982 on measures to facilitate the effective exercise of freedom of establishment and freedom to provide services in respect of activities of self-employed persons in certain services incidental to transport and travel agencies (ISIC Group 718) and in storage and warehousing (ISIC group 720) is also of relevance.

For guidance Article 3 lists, in respect of the activities listed in Article 2, the usual titles current in the Member States. In the United Kingdom they are: apart from tour operator, travel agent, air broker, and air travel organizer (group B); the titles of freight forwarder, ship broker, air cargo agent, shipping and forwarding agent (group A); storekeeper, livestock dealer, market or lairage operator, warehousekeeper, wharfinger (group C); motorvehicle examiner, master porter and cargo superintendent (group D).

In respect of group B Article 2 mentions the following activities:

- The organizing, offering for sale and selling, outright or on commission, single or collective items (transport, board, lodging, excursions etc.) for a journey or stay, whatever the reason for travelling;
- arranging, negotiating and concluding contracts for the transport of emigrants.

According to Article 1(2) this Directive shall also apply to nationals of the Member States who, as provided in Regulation 1612/68,[127] wish to pursue as employed persons activities coming within Article 2 of this Directive. In case C–306/89 (Commission v. Greece) the European Court held that by failing to adopt within the prescribed period the laws, regulations and administrative provisions required to comply with Directive 82/470/EEC Greece had failed to fulfil its obligations under the Treaty.[128]

Tourism and Energy

The initial guidelines, under the heading of 'Working conditions for those engaged in tourism', also made reference to energy matters.[129] Energy questions do affect tourism. The price of fuel has a considerable impact on transport costs and on costs of heating and air conditioning in hotels. The Commission from an early date felt that measures to limit the effects of momentary oil shortages are important to tourism. Unfortunately, the EC has not developed a proper comprehensive energy policy and it seems content with mere co-ordination of national measures. However, there are some measures in this sphere that are relevant to tourism such as the regulation on the basis of which the EC gives financial aid of between 25 and 49 per cent of their total costs to projects to exploit alternative energy sources.[130] The EC also grants financial support for demonstration projects in the field of energy saving.[131] Hotels, leisure centres, swimming pools, etc. have received assistance under these measures. Anyone interested can apply for such Community aid or obtain and use, on non-discriminatory commercial terms, the results of past projects financed by the EC.

INCREASING KNOWLEDGE OF TOURISM AND ORGANISATION OF CONSULTATION AND CO-OPERATION

There is a shortage of reliable information on tourism at EC level which prevents serious assessment of the present situation of tourism as well as its development. It is, moreover, considered necessary by the Commission to promote exchange of views and information between representatives of the Member States, specialist bodies and the Commission in order to facilitate co-ordination measures by the Member States and the development of EC policy.[132]

A consultation and co-operation procedure in the field of tourism was already established by Council Decision 86/664/EEC.[133] The EC's role in publishing statistics, opinions, surveys and information on tourism was stressed by the European Parliament[134] and on 30 May 1990 the Commission submitted a proposal for a Council Decision on the implementation of a multi-annual programme (1991 to 1993) for developing Community tourism statistics which has been adopted by the Council meanwhile.[135] On a unified market there is a need for reliable, speedy and comparable data based on EC criteria. It is, furthermore, felt that the business environment should be improved by better analysis and dissemination of information at Community level. There was a need for an EC reference framework for tourism statistics. At present statistical data available in the Member States are not comparable. The multi-annual programme aims to define and implement an EC frame for reference for EC statistics on tourism by the approximation of the concepts and methods already used by the Member States. The Commission is to analyse and evaluate the needs of the main users, analyse existing national systems, prepare an EC methodological framework for statistics and collect and disseminate data. By main users is understood EC institutions, national administrations, international organizations as well as economic operators. The analysis of existing national systems will comprise analyses of supply and demand, monitoring of EC development against that of the rest of the world and data from other statistical projects having a bearing on tourism. Member States will have to ascertain and analyse needs of the main national users and hold consultation meetings at national level. The Commission will co-ordinate these activities after consultation with the Statistical Programme Committee (which has already been established). There will be an obligation on the Member States to supply the Commission with existing statistics on tourism and on any information it may require on the methodology used for collecting such statistics.

This initiative, which must be welcomed, is overdue and will prove to be of great benefit to national and EC decision-makers, firms in the tourist industry and consumers alike. The framework will be used as a harmonization tool for the development of European statistics and as a recommended basis for non-official statistics. This EC statistical action plan, furthermore, aims to collect and regularly disseminate data on tourism. Surveys on holiday habits can also be quite useful, but the results of national surveys are not always comparable and are frequently not available outside the country in question. The Commission therefore wishes to encourage the harmonization of surveys and in 1986 carried out a first sample survey on the holidays of Europeans.[136]

The Commission has stressed that the complexities of the Tourism sector and its interaction with many other areas of economic activity mean that consultation and co-ordination between Member States and the Commission is essential.[137] This was also emphasized by the Council in its resolution of 10 April 1984 on a Community policy on tourism.[138] On 22 December 1986 the Council adopted the above-mentioned Decision establishing a consultation and co-operation procedure in the field of tourism.[139] A flexible procedure is available now to enable Member States to consult with each other and co-ordinate their activities. According to Article 3 of the Decision Member States must send to the Commission once a year a report on the most significant measures they have taken or intend to take in the sphere of tourism, which could have consequences for travellers from other Member States. Questions of common interest can be discussed in an (advisory) Tourism Committee which is to facilitate the exchange of information, consultation, and where appropriate co-operation on tourism and, in particular, on the provision of services for tourists. The Commission also wishes to develop its contacts with the industry. Apart from the work that has been done for harmonizing statistical data in the field of services, the Commission has completed the relevant surveys 'Amelioration of statistics in Tourism', referring to hotels, restaurants and cafes (HORECA) in 1988 and a more recent one referring to hotel characterization in the Member States in May 1989 (see Chapter 4). Finally a study on the establishment of a documentation centre which will gather information on all branches of tourism has been launched in order to facilitate the task of co-ordinating tourist data in a more homogeneous way.[140]

3

Actions Already Taken

One of the difficulties surrounding tourism is that it interacts with a multitude of other areas of economic activity, as was pointed out above, when the need for consultation and co-operation was discussed. The corollary of this is that several EC policies, programmes and measures without being directly geared towards tourism, already provide responses to the requirements of changing and developing tourist activities. The Commission's action plan to assist tourism distinguishes three types of programmes and measures:[1] first there are the general measures connected with the completion of the Internal Market; second there are actions resulting from the application of EC policies; and third there are direct measures in favour of tourism and actions undertaken as part of the European Year of Tourism.

GENERAL MEASURES RELATED TO THE COMPLETION OF THE INTERNAL MARKET

In general terms the development of EC case law and of EC legislation has brought changes in the economic and legal environment of tourism. Such changes are not exclusive to tourism but affect all sectors of the economy. Neverthless certain measures have a particular impact on or importance for tourism.

Transport

A notorious and self-evident example of a policy which affects tourism is transport. Tourism, by definition, involves mobility. The EC by its measures on transport, even if transport is not the best progressing file, has considerably assisted the development of tourism.[2] Road, rail and air links have improved beyond recognition. Motorways no longer stop a few miles from national frontiers. The completion of a true European Community in the field of transport is one of the priorities of the 1992 programme. Much will still have to be achieved in this area, however. For example, the current rules for air transport do not permit a system of fares which benefits the consumer. The complete opening up of markets is also difficult if not impossible under the present rules. The EEC Treaty has already devoted an entire title to transport (Article 74–84 EEC) providing for the elimination of discrimination and the establishment of a series of common rules. In 1961 the Commission issued a memorandum proposing measures to unify the European Market on the basis of the following principles: free competition; free choice of means of transport for the user; equal treatment for all forms of transport and all transport companies, public and private; financial and commercial independence for firms; co-ordination of infrastructures. Over the years the Council has adopted specific measures in areas such as: the rights of establishment for transporters; length of driving periods for those in charge of heavy goods vehicles; administrative independence for railway companies and co-operation between them; standards for ships, etc.[3] Neverthless, the Council was taken to court by the European Parliament and was censured by the Court of Justice in 1985 for not having fulfilled its duty to establish free circulation of transport services and abolish all discrimination based on nationality or place of establishment.[4] However, the Commission's White Paper on the completion of the Internal Market of the same year provided a new impetus. The completion of the Internal Market is an aim which encompasses the freedom to provide services in the transport sector. Once this market will be complete and one must hope that this is not too long after the end of 1992, every qualified transporter from a Member State should be able to offer services anywhere in the EC without having to be established in another Member State.[5]

Road, rail and air transport are clearly particularly important to tourism. An early measure in the sphere of road transport which has played a crucial role in the development of tourism within the EC, is Regulation No 117/66 on the introduction of common rules for international carriage of passengers by coach and bus, which provided that occasional coach and bus services should be exempt from the requirement of authorization by any Member State except the one where the vehicle is registered.[6] Another early Regulation established common rules for regular and special regular services by coach and bus between Member States.[7] It standardized the procedures for drawing up and issuing authorizations to operate such services and provided the authorities with means to check the development of the market. The Council also simplified the administrative formalities governing regular services between port areas served by a regular sea-transport service.[8]

In another Regulation the Council established common rules for shuttle services by coach and bus between Member States.[9] Therefore the EC's legislation already in an early stage was helpful as far as coach and bus services were concerned. Going beyond the EC there is the ASOR agreement which provides for common rules covering regular and/or shuttle coach and bus services between the EC and a number of third countries such as Austria, Finland, Norway, Sweden, Switzerland and Turkey.[10]

The proposal for a Council Regulation on common rules for international carriage of passengers by coach and bus, is also relevant to tourism. It aims to:

- introduce the freedom to provide road passenger transport services on journeys within the Community;
- to review the rules governing this sector;
- enforce road safety.[11]

Another proposal of importance for tourism is currently before the Council for adoption. It is the proposal for a Council Regulation laying down the conditions under which non-resident carriers may operate national road passenger transport services within a Member State. It aims to enable non-resident carriers to have the freedom to provide national transport services within a Member State without discrimination on grounds of nationality or place of establishment.[12] There is also legislation in respect of qualifications. The occupation of road haulage operator and road passenger transport operator is the subject of Directives 74/561 and 74/562.[13] Good repute, appropriate financial standing and technical competence are required for the exercise of these occupations. There is also a Directive (77/796) on mutual recognition of diplomas and other evidence of qualifications for such operators. Directive 89/438, which amended these three Directives, aims to encourage the effectiveness of operators.[14]

Other transport legislation is concerned with vehicle standards such as the weights, dimensions and other technical features of vehicles.[15] Since 1970 a Tachograph has had to be installed in lorries and buses to record lengths of driving periods, compulsory rest periods (which are now harmonized) and driving speeds.[16] Pending the total abolition of borders the Commission aims, as seen above, to ease the procedures for international coach and bus passenger services.[17]

Rail transport

Rail transport is of considerable importance to tourism. The rail network has gradually been improved; the tourist market has broadenend and caters now also for those with more modest means. The development of high-speed international passenger services will also benefit tourism.

The Commission and the European Parliament are in favour of the development of a European high-speed rail network. The Commission put forward a global plan in November 1989 to place the railways on a sounder footing and to enable them to make use of their advantages in the context of the single market.[18] The Economic and Social Committee meanwhile has generally approved the Commission's proposals in respect of a common rail policy, albeit with some criticism of certain aspects of the draft Directive on the development of railways in the EC.[19] The Commission's communication on a common rail policy is accompanied not only by the mentioned proposed Council Directive but also by proposals for:

- a Council Regulation amending Regulation 1191/69/EEC on action in connection with public service obligations in the field of transport by rail, road and inland waterway;
- a Council Decision on the establishment of a European high-speed rail network;
- a Council Directive amending Directive 75/130/EEC on the establishment of common rules for certain combined rail/road goods traffic between Member States.[20]

The Commission aims for a European rail policy, gradual integration of networks and dismantling of monopolies. The proposed measures seek to establish a general framework for railways. Railway transport will, of course, be greatly improved by high-speed trains and big infrastructure projects such as the Channel tunnel.

Air transport

From the perspective of tourism the most important changes in transport are related to air transport. Of particular relevance are the proposals of December 1987 on the liberalization of the industry.[21] The measures are concerned with matters such as passenger capacity, market access and fares.[22] Furthermore, two important Regulations have been adopted in respect of computerized reservation systems.[23] Another welcome Regulation is Council Regulation EEC No 295/91 of 4 February 1991 establishing common rules for a denied boarding compensation system in scheduled air transport.[24] For a long time the Commission has rightly considered that the general level of tariffs among regular airlines was too high. Even if charter transport had strengthened and had caused price competition between charter companies, this changed little with regard to scheduled flights. The Commission has from an early date been in favour of the establishment of an efficient European network which would not be hindered by national barriers, and already in 1979 in its memorandum of 4 July on the EC's contribution to the development of air transport services, it proposed changes in the tariff structure of regular services to provide more attractive fares for the tourist market and for interregional transport.[25]

Although some competition had already been introduced to many regional airports, the 1987 measures constituted a significant breakthrough.[26] The measures provided for:

- more flexibility in the sharing of capacity and access to routes;
- relaxation of pricing rules. Carriers are no longer obliged to align their fares with those of their competitors. (The right of governments to oppose the introduction of new fares has been limited particularly in respect of low fares for off-peak periods and for certain categories of passengers.)
- the application to air traffic of the EC's competition rules, with exemptions being allowed only for agreements indispensable to the co-ordination of services.

In case 66/86 the ECJ held that bilateral or multilateral agreements fixing tariffs for international flights between EC airports unless exempted by the Commission were automatically void under EC law.[27] The conditions for exemption were laid down in Regulation 3975/87.[28] The Court also held that the prohibitions contained in Article 86 EEC were fully applicable to the air transport sector. The Court had already ruled that the Treaty provisions on competition apply to transport.[29]

Apart from the second phase proposals on capacity, access and fares the Commission has also made proposals for a coherent civil aviation policy dealing with such matters as safety measures, air traffic congestion, recognition of diplomas and qualifications. In June 1990 it, furthermore, proposed to establish EC competence in respect of a common approach in dealings with third countries.[30]

Licensing of air carriers and other developments in air transport

In Council Regulation (EEC) No 2343/90[31] the Council already decided to adopt for implementation before 1 July 1992 rules governing the licensing of air carriers. It was seen as important to define non-discriminatory requirements in relation to the location and control of the undertaking applying for a licence. The Commission has meanwhile put forward a proposal for a Council Regulation on licensing of air carriers.[32] It is considered important that carriers at all times operate at sound economical and high safety levels, that in view of the protection of the consumer air carriers are properly insured against liability risks and that the granting of licences to carriers should be transparent and non-discriminatory. The draft is concerned with the economic and technical competence requirements for the grant and retention of operational licences and air operators certificates. No company shall be permitted within the EC to carry passengers mail and or cargo for remuneration and or hire without the appropriate licence and air operators certificate (a document confirming that the operator is competent to secure the safe operation of his aircraft).

The Commission has also issued a proposal concerning access.[33] The first steps for air carriers to scheduled intra-Community air-routes to ensure the Internal Market were already made by Decision 87/602/EEC[34] and Regulation (EEC) 2343/90.[35] The Regulation needed revision. The draft deals with access to routes between airports within the EC for both scheduled and non-scheduled air services. A third draft in the sphere of aviation deals with air fares and rates.[36]. The groundwork in this field was already done in Council Directive 87/601/EEC[37] and Council Regulation (EEC) No 2342/90.[38] The thinking is that fares should normally be determined freely by market forces, where competition exists, and that where competition is limited it is appropriate to provide for a transparent and objective procedure which enables the Member States to ask the Commission to examine and decide whether a proposed air fare conforms with the criteria laid down. This measure is concerned with the criteria and procedures to be applied for the establishment of air fares and rates charged by air carriers on air services within the EC.

According to the draft, Member States may not disapprove air fares and rates of Community air carriers if they are reasonably related to the applicant air carrier's long-term fully-allocated relevant costs, while taking into account the need for a satisfactory return on capital and for an adequate cost margin to ensure a satisfactory safety standard. In disapproving air fares Member States must also take into account the needs of consumers, the competitive market situation, the fares of other air carriers operating on the route and the need to prevent dumping. The fact that a proposed fare is lower than that of another EC air carrier operating on the same route will not be a sufficient ground for withholding approval. Carriers may not charge fares or rates that are excessively high to the disadvantage of users or unjustifiably low in view of the competitive market situation. Only EC air carriers will be entitled to introduce lower fares than the existing ones. Air fares offered to tour operators or offered to the public specifically combined with accommodation for the duration of the trip and fares for groups larger than six persons will be automatically approved.

The above measures not only represent important building blocks for the completion of the Internal Market and the EC's transport policy but are also of great relevance to consumers, the tourist trade and the business world in general.

Transport Infrastructure

It would almost be tautological to state that transport infrastructure is crucial to tourism. It is after all via roads and motorways that tourists reach their destination. As pointed out above, several Community instruments have contributed towards the financing of transport infrastructure projects. In 1988 the EIB loaned 1,600 million ECU for the improvement of transport infrastructure in the EC.[39] The European Regional Development Fund provided a similar amount in non-refundable grants for the same purpose.

The Commission feels that it is crucial to define a network of transport infrastructure to the development of which the EC would financially contribute. It has drawn up a programme which focuses on the needs of the large Internal Market of 1992. The aim is to integrate the various national networks, eliminate several bottlenecks, serve peripheral areas, improve links between the main urban centres and improve transit conditions through Switzerland, Austria and Yugoslavia.

Taxation

Apart from transport there are other measures in the context of the completion of the Internal Market that have a bearing on tourism. One set of these consists of the measures concerning taxation.

In chapter 2 in the context of police and tax checks reference has already been made to tax harmonization. The Commission wishes to abolish fiscal frontiers. Proposals specifically affecting tourism relate to transport of passengers within and between Member States which the Commission has proposed to be taxed in the Country of departure. The Commission also proposed to abolish from January 1993 tax-free purchases between Member States and the limits on the quantity and value of taxed purchases. In other words, tax-free allowances for persons travelling between Member States will, therefore, completely disappear.[40] It has been estimated that the effect of discontinuing duty-free shopping for travellers will be a 2.2 billion ECU drop in turnover in duty-free goods.[41] The figure for intra-Community travel would be 1.4 billion ECU. The Commission, however, does not accept these figures since it feels that they are based on the wrong assumptions and that the effects on fares of the ending of tax and duty-free shopping in intra-EC travel should not be estimated in isolation. In the Commission's view, account should be taken of the dynamic effect that the introduction of an integrated Internal Market will have and of the general development of transport infrastructure.

In its harmonization of legislation on turnover taxes the EC has always given special attention to the hotel trade and the problems of travel agents. It was decided, for example, that the agent's profit alone should be eligible for VAT.[42] A remaining problem was the variation in rates across the EC. The European Parliament has expressed the view that fiscal harmonization will on the whole make tourism cheaper, since transport, food and drink, energy, cultural goods and services would be taxed according to the lower rate.[43] However, the tax measures of the 1992 programme have been criticized by the ESC as counter-productive for tourism.[44] There is a fear that such measures could increase rates for intra-Community transport and thus discriminate in favour of extra-EC transport links. It was pointed out that tax harmonization could also affect hotels and tourist facilities and have a negative effect on employment.

The Commission was urged to promote in the run-up to 1992 a campaign to abolish VAT or reduce it to a minimum in respect of hotels, thermal resorts, rural tourism and restaurants, in order to defend and safeguard these sectors from unfair competition from third countries.[45] In 1990 the Commission, in answer to questions raised in the European Parliament, explained its position on VAT on hotel catering services.[46] Its tax proposals provided for a reduced rate of tax (4 to 9 per cent) on foodstuffs and a standard rate (14 to 19 per cent) on hotel and catering services. The Commission pointed out that in drawing up the list of goods and services to be covered by the proposed lower rate of VAT, it was guided by the practice prevailing in most Member States. It seems that only one Member State applies the standard rate to foodstuffs in general. The rules with regard to hotels and catering, however, are not so clear cut. Some Member States which do tax them at a lower rate, nevertheless impose restrictions on the type and class of establishment which may qualify. Therefore, for the sake of clarity and simplicity of the VAT system, the Commission did not propose that hotels and catering industry should be included under the lower rate. It appears that seven Member States (i.e. Luxembourg, The Netherlands, Greece, Portugal, Ireland, Italy and Spain) do apply reduced rates to the catering industry.

The Commission explained that its approach to the harmonization of indirect taxes was to propose the minimum number of changes in the national fiscal systems consistent with the abolition of fiscal frontiers in line with Article 99 EEC as amended by the Single European Act. While trying to avoid going against other EC policies, the objective of completing the Internal Market had overriding priority for the Commission which was asked, in particular, whether it had considered the implications for the employment situation in the hotel and catering industry of applying a standard rate of VAT in those Member States which at present apply a reduced rate. Meanwhile, during the Luxembourg Presidency important developments have taken place regarding harmonization of indirect taxation.[47] On 24 June 1991, at last, agreements were reached on the levels of VAT and excise duty rates to be applied in the EC from January 1993. The Luxembourg Presidency had, unlike the Commission, put forward a package of compromise proposals advocating merely minimum rates for VAT and excise duty. The Commission's proposals, as pointed out above, were based on both minimum and maximum rates.

The Member States came to a political agreement that from 1 January 1993 they apply a minimum standard rate of VAT of 15 per cent. It was furthermore agreed that there should be one or two optional reduced VAT rates of not less than 5 per cent to be applied to an agreed list of goods and services such as food, passenger transport, books and newspapers. The finance ministers came also to an agreement, in principle, to move toward an origin based system of taxation from 1 January 1997. Under such a system goods will be taxed before dispatch at the rate of the Member State from which they are sent.

With regard to excise duties agreement was reached on specific minimum rates for petrol, diesel, heavy oil, beer and cigarettes. A Directive on this matter is in the pipeline. A provisional agreement was reached on a minimum rate of zero for wine, heating kerosene and heating gas oil pending the outcome of a Commission Report on a satisfactory control system. A minimum rate for spirits was left to be decided later. The Commission agreed to study the effects of differing excise rates on the alcoholic drinks market. These agreements must be welcomed: they will enable both the EC and businesses to plan for the abolition of fiscal frontiers.

During the Dutch Presidency further progress was made in respect of fiscal barriers.[48] A Directive was adopted on VAT technical arrangements to apply after 1992 and political agreement was reached on a Regulation providing for administrative co-operation as well as on a draft Directive on the arrangements for the holding, movement and control of goods subject to excise duty. It was also decided to retain duty-free shopping until 1997.

The VAT technical system Directive will amend the sixth VAT directive and introduce the concept of 'acquisition' to replace imports as the taxable event for intra-EC transactions. During a transitional period the 'destination system' will apply to all supplies between traders registered for VAT. Tax will be paid on acquisition of goods in the receiving states. There is also provision for special schemes that extend above set thresholds the destination system to supplies between traders registered for VAT and private non-registered bodies. This applies to distance selling, sales of new boats, aircraft and motor vehicles and purchases by exempt bodies and private individuals. All other purchases by private individuals and unregistered traders and exempt bodies will be made tax-paid in the State of purchase. This is known as the origin system. Under the Directive on excisable goods, goods will be taxed under the destination principle, i.e. they will be liable to duty in the state of consumption, with the exception of goods brought in from another Member State by private travellers for their own personal use. Meanwhile, the Economic and Finance Ministers agreed a plan whereby the current duty free allowances will not be phased out until July 1999. Excise duties still need to be harmonized, but political agreement has been reached that the minimum standard rate of VAT will be 15 per cent and the existing zero rates will be continued.[49]

Company law

The EC's proposals on company law are also of major importance for the tourist trade. The Commission, in the context of the completion of the Internal Market, is concentrating its efforts on the creation of a Community framework rather than a strictly national framework for company law. For example, there is the proposal for a fifth company law Directive which is aimed at closer harmonization of national law.[50] Another proposal of relevance for tourism is the proposal for a tenth company law Directive on the removal of legal obstacles to cross-border mergers.[51] Another relevant draft is the proposal for a thirteenth Directive on the harmonization of procedures to be followed with regard to take-overs and other general bids.[52]

Apart from harmonizing national laws the EC is also in the process of developing specific Community instruments such as the EEIG (European Economic Interest Grouping). This is a new method of transnational co-operation which has been available to business since July 1989.[53] For instance a plan has been developed for an EEIG between five of the Main European Tourism Fairs.[54] The 'Cooperation Fairs' project is aimed at transferring to the tourism sector the experience gained in the industry sector in particular for small and medium-sized enterprises through the Europartnerhip projects.[55] Europartnership operations aim to make the best possible use of the potential in underdeveloped regions by promoting co-operation agreements between firms in the region and companies elsewhere in the EC.[56] Such projects have already been successful in Ireland, Andalusia and Wales.

Another example of an EC instrument is the statute for a European company which will enable companies to co-operate by the setting up of a European company (by merger, by the formation of a holding company or by the formation of a joint subsidiary). A European company will operate under the provisions of the European company statute, which will cover most areas of company law.[57]

Establishment and Freedom to Provide Services

In Chapter 2 reference was made to legislation in respect of the freedom to provide services and the right of establishment as well as to the introduction of a general system for the recognition of qualifications (see p. 36).

Competition Policy

Another policy which increasingly has a bearing on tourism and on firms in the travel trade is the EC's competition policy. The European Court has had to deal with matters such as: contracts concluded between a tour operator and a travel agent; agreements obliging travel agents to invoice the prices set by operators for package tours or prohibiting them from passing on to customers some of the commission they receive for the sale of holidays or from granting discounts to customers; exclusive distribution and exclusive purchasing agreements, whereby a travel agent is obliged to purchase holidays from a particular operator only or not to sell holidays proposed by competitors.[58]

In case 311/85[59] the Court held that legislative provisions or regulations of a Member State requiring travel agents to observe the prices and tariffs for travel set by tour operators, prohibiting them from sharing the commission paid in respect of the sale of such travel with the customers or granting them rebates and regarding such acts as contrary to fair trading practice are incompatible with Articles 5, 3(f) and 85 EEC, where the object or effect of such national legislation is to reinforce the effect of agreements, decisions or concerted practices which are contrary to Article 85.

The Court concluded that there was a whole network of agreements in the industry, both between travel agents themselves and between travel agents and tour operators, the object or effect of which was to compel travel agents to observe the prices set by the operators. The aim was to restrict competition between agents. The Court did not accept, as was suggested by the Belgian government, that a travel agent could be described as an auxiliary organ forming an integral part of a tour operator's undertaking. Under Belgian law tour operators could bring actions for unfair competition against price cutters. Belgian law not only gave such an anti-competitive system permanent effect but also extended it to non participating firms and provided penalties for those that passed on their commission.

In another case two Frankfurt travel agents, Ahmed Saeed and Silver Line, offered travellers air tickets for the Lisbon–Frankfurt–Tokyo route. The tickets had been bought in London. The clients only took the Frankfurt–Tokyo flight and in the process saved up to 60 per cent of the price of a normal Frankfurt–Tokyo ticket bought in Germany. The agents were taken to court by an association fighting unfair competition (Zentrale zur Bekämpfung Unlauteren Wettbewerbs) for having infringed German law which prescribed that only tariffs approved by German law might be applied in Germany. They were also accused of unfair competition since the tickets they sold undercut the approved tariffs. The lower courts ruled against the travel agents. The Bundesgerichthof agreed with the lower courts on the points of law but referred the matter to Luxembourg for a ruling of the ECJ on the compatibility of the relevant German law with EC law. The European Court held not only that bilateral or multilateral agreements fixing tariffs for international flights between EC airports, unless exempted by the Commission, were automatically void under EC law, but also that Article 86 (prohibiting the abuse of dominant positions) was fully applicable to the air transport sector.[60] The Court further held that national authorities were not allowed to facilitate the conclusion of tariff agreements contrary to Articles 85 and 86.

During the written procedure of this case the Court had delivered another important ruling.[61] in which it held that the Treaty provisions on competition did in principle apply to transport. The Court had been asked whether it would be against EC law to prosecute a travel agent who had charged fares below the tariff imposed by French law, if the tariff itself infringed Articles 85 and 86 EEC.

Since Asjes several Regulations have been adopted applying EC competition rules to air transport and laying down procedures and sanctions (see Chapter 3, p. 47). On 30 November 1988 the Commission adopted Regulation 4087/88 on franchise agreements[62] which came into effect on 1 February 1989.[63]

Franchise agreements are often used by tour operators and travel agents and could be of use to other actors on the tourist scene, such as hotels. Another example of an important measure in the sphere of competition which applies, of course, to mergers in the tourist sector is the merger control Regulation which was adopted on 21 December 1989.[64]

Social Action Programme

In 1990, after the adoption by eleven of the Member States of the Community Charter of Fundamental Social Rights of Workers, the Commission initiated work on an action programme relating to the implementation of the Charter of basic social rights, which complements the economic aspects of the completion of the Internal Market.[65] Several of the proposals of this action programme are relevant to tourism. This is in particular the case in respect of the proposed Directives on atypical work. The Commission has adopted three draft Directives in this field and wishes to create minimum rules in this increasingly important area.[66]

Currently there are 14 million part-time wage earners and some 10 million workers are employed on an interim or time-limited basis in the EC. Often this type of contract, given its flexibility, is of interest not only to the employees but also to the businesses concerned. Many activities in the tourist industry, given the type of work and, in particular, given its inherent seasonal character, may be covered by these proposals and the proposal on the adaptation of working time. The first draft, on working conditions, seeks to guarantee part-time workers and temporary staff working more than eight hours per week access to vocational training and social service benefits. It further provides for comparable treatment to full-time workers in relation to social assistance and non-contributory social security. According to the second draft, on avoiding distortion of competition, Member States must ensure that such workers are subject to the same legal and professional social security systems as full-time staff. Annual leave, redundancy benefits and seniority must also be guaranteed. The objective of the third Directive is to guarantee temporary staff the same health and safety conditions as apply to other workers. The European Parliament has asked the Commission to make specific proposals to apply the principles of the proposal on atypical work to cover seasonal workers in the tourist industry having regard to their particular needs and circumstances and it has urged the Member States and the Commission to undertake work on better vocational training of seasonal staff.[67]

In addition to these draft Directives on atypical work there is a draft on flexible working hours.[68] This proposal includes *inter alia* rules on minimum rest periods, annual paid leave, night working, etc. The adaptation, flexibility and organization of working time are important not only for the workers concerned but also for the dynamism of firms and those in the tourist, hotel and catering trades, in particular.

There are also other proposals which are more general in scope but which could nevertheless be relevant to tourism. One of these is the proposal on information, consultation and participation of workers in businesses or in groups of businesses with a Community dimension.[69] There is also a proposal for a Directive on written declarations relating to employment relationships.[70] This proposal seeks to ensure that workers who are not covered by a written contract or letter of engagement should be provided with a written declaration setting out details of the terms applicable to the work concerned.

A final example are the proposals on the living and working conditions of EC citizens living in border areas, in particular frontier workers, and on minimum rules to protect workers posted to another EC Country.[71] As a result of the agreement (or lack of it) reached at Maastricht in December 1991 the social dimension will have little direct relevance for the United Kingdom and UK business, at least for the time being. However, the effect of legislation based on the existing EEC treaty and the Single European Act will, of course, remain unchanged.

ACTION RESULTING FROM EC POLICIES

The EC's enterprise policy which places information, co-operation, financing and training instruments at the disposal of businesses has an indirect effect on tourism.[72]. The economic base of the tourism sector is essentially composed of small and medium-sized firms (SMEs). Firms in the tourist, hotel and catering business, therefore, have an interest in following the developments in the sphere of enterprise policy and SMEs.[73]

The Commission aims to bring about a 'quantum leap' to assist SMEs in facing up to the post 1992 situation. It has adopted new enterprise guidelines in support of enterprises and SMEs in particular.[74] The focus will be on creation of the right environment, increased information and development of co-operation between firms. Enterprise policy will develop along the lines of the Euro-info centres, the Business Cooperation Network (BC-Net) and partnership. Each proposed law must now be accompanied by a description of its likely effects on competitiveness and employment. In November 1986 it was decided to transmit to the Council an impact assessment statement with each legislative proposal.[75] This is not only of great importance for the business world, in general, but there is also an interesting positive spin-off for tourism since this procedure for evaluating the impact of proposed measures on smaller firms makes it also relatively easy to identify the areas of EC activities that have a tourist dimension. In particular the following areas have already been identified as such: regional policy, consumer protection, measures to develop rural areas, cultural development in the EC, environment policy, and education and training.[76] In most of these action has already been taken to assist tourism in the EC.

Regional Policy

The EC, in the context of its regional policy, sees tourism as one of the economic sectors that could assist in developing the poorer regions. Between 1986 and 1988 about 5 per cent of the ERDF was allocated to projects for the development of tourism. The percentage was even greater in respect of certain programmes such as the IMPs.[77] Following the reform of the structural funds, the EC support frameworks for 1989–93 include the promotion of tourism: 5.5 per cent or 1.6 billion ECU for regions whose development is lagging behind (objective 1 regions). In the EC support framework for regions whose development is lagging behind specific priorities for the expansion of tourism have been proposed and they qualify for a considerable financial contribution from the EC. For Ireland,

Spain and Greece 188.6 million ECU, 182 million ECU and 166.7 million ECU, respectively have been allocated to tourism.[78]

For objective 5b (rural development) the figure is 176 million ECU. With regard to regional conversion (objective 2) the EC support frameworks provide 267 million ECU for tourism activities in the period 1989–91. To this must be added loans from the EIB for tourist infrastructure (see Chapter 2).

Consumer Policy

Several measures have been taken in the sphere of consumer protection. An outstanding example is the Directive on package holidays which, given its crucial nature, will be discussed separately in Chapter 4.[79] Another example (in the sphere of transport) is the adoption by the Council of a Regulation establishing common rules for a denied-boarding compensation system in scheduled air transport.[80]

Tourists as consumers will also be protected under the Directive on unfair terms in consumer contracts.[81] The proposal for this Directive sets out a list of unfair terms that will be prohibited in contracts between suppliers and consumers as purchasers of goods and services. The objective is to place all consumers in the EC on the same footing and to protect those crossing borders to make purchases or to contract for services.

Rural Development

As pointed out in Chapter 2 various EC measures are available to the rural tourism business, particularly under the CAP[82] Council Regulation EEC No 797/85[83] on improving the efficiency of agricultural structures, as amended by Regulation No 3808/89, provides for aid which extends to investment in tourist and craft activities on farms. The scheme may be applied to farmers who derive at least 50 per cent of their total income from activities carried out on the holding. However, the proportion of income coming directly from farming may not be less than 25 per cent of the farmer's total income and off-farm activities may not account for more than half the farmers working time.[84]

Agritourism measures limited to specific areas can also be taken under Council Regulation (EEC) No 1820/80 for the stimulation of agricultural development in the less favoured areas in the west of Ireland[85] or under Council Regulation (EEC) No 1401/86 introducing a common action for the encouragement of agriculture in certain less favoured areas of Italy and certain Scottish Islands.[86]

The EC initiative for rural development LEADER has already been mentioned in chapter 2.[87]. There is another programme called LEDA (Local Employment Development Action research programme set up by DGV of the Commission) which organizes exchanges of development experience at European level. It evaluates those possibilities which will stimulate the rural fabric and assist employment by the promotion of activities linked to tourism. Furthermore, the Community support frameworks provide for action to promote rural tourism and vocational training in the field of tourism including the financing of investment in tourist facilities, such as farm accommodation and the development of nature parks, or sport complexes (e.g. golf, skiing). A number of priority measures have already been highlighted.[88]

Cultural Development

As was pointed out in Chapter 2 the Commission has identified cultural tourism as one of the main spheres of EC action. In its 1987 communication on matters of culture it identified several areas that could be of interest in this context, such as:

- support for pilot projects relating to the conservation of the architectural heritage;
- actions relating to European cities of culture;
- a programme to encourage cultural events with a European dimension.[89]

Since 1990, these matters have been streamlined and publicized under the heading 'Platform Europe'. During the European Year of Tourism[90] support was given to several pan-European projects for the creation of European cultural itineraries for tourists. These routes have been worked out at the initiative of the Council of Europe[91]. The ministers, responsible for cultural affairs, taking into account the work accomplished by the Council of Europe and the potential role of the European Foundation in this field, agreed both to stimulate activities in the field of transnational cultural itineraries by encouraging the Member States to co-operate across frontiers in the study and possible development of itineraries of European interest and to leave such co-operation open to the other European countries. They also noted that such schemes might be eligible for support from the various existing Community instruments.

Environmental Policy

There is also increasing concern that tourism should develop in harmony with the environment. As the opinion of the ESC on tourism and regional development of 1990 puts it, the typical holiday on the beach in the sun, on the ski slopes or elsewhere has led to overcrowding, over-exploitation and depletion of resources for tourism in many regions, causing major environmental and cultural impoverishment.[92]

The ESC has suggested a new approach which takes note of past mistakes in respect of destruction of the ecological balance and overloading of installed facilities and leads to investment in infrastructure especially environmental infrastructure in resorts hit by the crisis in growth.[93] It further backs the development of abovementioned alternative forms of tourism (see Chapter 2) and advocates regulations to preserve and raise standards. The ESC asks for support for refurbishment of old hotel accommodation and restoration of old buildings for tourist accommodation and other facilities. In other words long-term interest must take priority over shortterm expediency. The concern for tourism to take the environment adequately into account is also reflected in the European Parliament's resolution of 14 July 1990 on the measures to protect the environment from potential damage caused by mass tourism.[94]

The Commission for its part sees to it that in implementing the reform of the structural funds, Member States take into consideration the environmental impact of investment projects proposed for EC finance. EC funds now must be used to support projects that are in accordance with EC policy and that on the environment, in particular. The funds can aid protection of environmental resources that are directly linked to the economic development of eligible regions. The Commission has identified several fields of action that can contribute to this such as LEADER (liaison between rural development agencies)[95] and ENVIREG which is the regional action programme concerning the environment.[96] Among the Commission's priorities are action on pollution of coastal areas and management of hazardous and toxic industrial waste. The environmental situation is particularly disturbing in the Mediterranean, where coastal areas have seen rapid growth in both tourism and industry. Several EC environmental measures have or will have an impact on tourism. For example there is important legislation on environmental assessment.[97] Another obvious example is the Directive on the quality of bathing water.[98] Waste management, control of industrial and other emissions are, of course, also relevant to tourism.[99] The Commission has also issued a Green Paper on the Urban Environment in which it stresses the need to develop a planning strategy for urban tourism.[100]

The main environmental threat is apparently the private motor car. There are 120 million of them in the EC to pollute our cities, in which 80 per cent of the population (i.e. 250 million persons) live. The number of cars is expected to increase by 20 per cent over the next twenty years. London's traffic, in particular, needs to be looked at. The successful purification of the Thames and reduction of smog are insufficient. If more is not done noise pollution, atmospheric pollution and pollution of monuments will not decrease. Apart from cars, there is heating, waste and used water to pollute our cities. In order to prepare this Green Paper city management officials in cities such as Cardiff, Brussels, Rome, Avignon and Bremen were consulted. Progress is being made in respect of cleaner cars and lorries[101]. Water management will also have to be tackled: the situation is particularly poor in cities such as Naples, Brussels and Milan (not unimportant cities from the point of view of tourism). Other measures suggested are the protection of green zones and the protection of monuments. The Commission is also studying the use of economic and fiscal instruments in the EC environment policy and has found considerable support for this in the ESC which has come out in favour of such taxes.[102]

Education and Training

Major resources have been made available in the Member States for training in the field of tourism.[103] The Commission also has stepped up and diversified its work in respect of training. The reform of the structural funds has emphasized the relationship between training programmes and development needs. Therefore, programmes in the tourism sector, funded by several sources, are implemented in many Objective 1 regions (regions which are seriously lagging behind) where tourism development is a priority. Training in rural tourism has been tackled under Objective 5b (modernizing agriculture). More resources have been available in recent years for the European Social Funds traditional activities and special programmes have been implemented involving transnational co-operation, promotion of mobility and exchange of students and teaching staff and exchange of experience.[104] The subject of vocational training in the tourist industry has been intensively studied and pilot projects are being drawn up covering tourism and regional development in objective 1 and 5b areas as well as skills and improved access to further training in industry. In the context of EC policies such as the environment policy and enterprise policy some interesting experiments have been developed. For example, the Commission adopted an action programme to prepare managers of small and medium-sized businesses for 1992.[105]

DIRECT MEASURES IN FAVOUR OF TOURISM AND ACTIONS IN THE FRAMEWORK OF THE EUROPEAN YEAR OF TOURISM

Direct Measures

In 1984 the Council, by a Resolution of 10 April, took note of the Commission's communication setting out initial guidelines for an EC policy on tourism.[106] It also called on the Commission to put forward proposals to facilitate tourism in the EC based on consultations with the Member States and respecting the peculiarities of national policies as well as international commitment of the Member States. The Commission subsequently identified in its communication on Community action in the field of tourism the six main themes of EC action that were discussed in Chapter 2 (assistance, better distribution, better use of aid, information and protection, better working conditions, and increased awareness, consultation and co-operation).[107]

In December 1986 the Council adopted a recommendation on standardized information in hotels.[108] (This measure will be discussed in Chapter 4.) In the same year the Council adopted a recommendation on fire safety in hotels.[109] The Council furthermore adopted a resolution on a better seasonal and geographical distribution of tourism, the concept of which was extensively discussed in Chapter 2.[110] In its resolution the Council expressed its determination to do all in its power to achieve a better seasonal and geographical distribution of tourist activities within the EC and it invited the Member States to encourage the lengthening of tourist seasons, better staggering of holidays and publicity campaigns to promote staggered holidays. The Member States were furthermore invited to create alternative tourist destinations. Member States were also asked to notify the Commission of school holidays dates and (if possible) traffic forecasts, especially in respect of saturation of road infrastructure so that the Commission could disseminate such information. Finally, the Member States were invited to collaborate with one another and the Commission to co-ordinate efforts to achieve a better distribution of tourism. In Chapter 2 (p. 42) reference was made to the creation of the advisory Committee on tourism:[111] this decision made available to the Commission a useful instrument for co-operation with the Member States. The Committee is chaired by the Commission, which also provides the secretarial services. The Committee must meet at least once a year.

Actions in the Framework of the European Year of Tourism

In recognition of the importance of the tourist industry, which accounts for over 5 per cent of the EC's GDP, the Council decided that the year 1990 should be declared European Year of Tourism (EYT).[112]After the Commission's initial guidelines and its Communication on EC action of 1986, in November 1987 the Commission organized a conference on 'Tourism: horizon 1992' involving both public and private operators in the industry, which produced a considerable degree of agreement on the Commission's actions and aims. This consensus was confirmed by the Member States at meetings of ministers responsible for tourism in Glückburg in 1988 and in Rhodes in September 1988.[113] The involvement of the EP in the development of a policy on tourism should not be overlooked either: it has been very favourable towards an EC commitment in the tourism sector and on 22 January 1988 it adopted a Resolution on the facilitation, promotion and financing of tourism in the European Community.[114] In this Resolution the parliament not only drew attention to the overall importance of tourism to the European economy and to the need for more active EC involvement, but in point 7 of the resolution it proposed that 1990 be designated 'European Year of the Traveller'. The Commission took up this suggestion and presented it to the Council, which in December 1988 decided to declare 1990 'European Year of Tourism' and to set up a Steering Committee.[115]

Objectives
The objectives were: (a) to prepare for the establishment of a large area without frontiers turning the integrating role of tourism to account in the creation of a People's Europe; (b) to stress the economic and social importance of the tourism sector, *inter alia* in regional policy and job creation. To this end the Council decided to undertake or support co-ordinated actions of the EC, the Member States and private organizations from the tourist industry with the following aims:

- to promote greater knowledge among the citizens, and young people in particular, of the cultures and lifestyles of other Member States;
- to promote a better distribution (as described in Chapter 2) while respecting the quality of the environment, in particular by the staggering of holidays and the development of alternatives to mass tourism and of new destinations and new forms of Tourism;
- to promote intra-Community tourism, in particular by facilitating the movement of travellers and tourism from third countries to Europe.

Organization
To organize and co-ordinate the year, a Management Unit, comprising national experts from the Member States and consultants was created within the Tourism Unit of DG XXIII of the Commission.[116] The Unit was assisted by a network of part-time correspondents in the EC offices of the Member States. The Commission was aided by a Steering Committee composed of representatives from the Member States. Representatives of the EFTA countries were also invited to the meetings. Observers from the major tourism associations participated in the work of the Committee as observers. There were also national committees.[117] The Council Decision identified several types of actions:[118]

- actions without financial implications for the EC budget such as logo promotion, price reductions in transport and accommodation during the low season;
- action co-financed by the EC budget; co-financing of pilot projects, aimed at promoting off-season tourism, youth tourism, rural tourism, cultural, social and other forms of tourism; 269

projects out of more than 600 received were approved, representing 3,599.870 ECU;[119]

- actions financed solely by the EC budget, such as competitions, information and PR campaigns, administrative expenses and promotional material, ceremonies and the 'Eurotourism' bulletin.

Promotion

Promotional activities included the distribution of material in thirteen languages of the eighteen participating countries and public relation exercises. An interesting example of a public relations activity concerned the high profile EYT achieved in the context of the 1990 Eurovision Song Contest broadcast to a worldwide audience of 1 billion viewers. Each song was preceded by a video showing European tourist destinations and the objectives of EYT were explained by the commentator against the backdrop of a giant video-wall showing the EYT logo.[120] Another example is the series of programmes on European Tourism which CIRCOM (Coopérative Internationale de Recherche et d'Action en Matière de Communication) has started to make. CIRCOM is an organization representing virtually all European regional TV stations. The programmes will contain an overview of country or area with practical information and images of the tourist attractions. About twenty programmes will be produced in co-operation with EYT.

Furthermore, there were contacts with the press, sponsorship, competitions and tourism trade fairs. Meanwhile, a plan has been developed for an EEIG (European Economic Interest Grouping) between five of the main Community fairs. Such an EEIG could become one of the main actors in the European tourist industry and a useful partner of the Commission in promoting European tourism. There were also thematic monthly activities and even a balloon tour. The American Express organization assisted with research, publicity and conferences. The thematic monthly activities aimed to highlight specific outdoor activities such as horseriding, fishing, cycling and rural tourism.

Priority activities

Forty projects were selected in the sphere of youth tourism.[121] The Eurotrain project was the most successful youth exchange programme. A train bringing together more than 100 students from twenty-seven countries, travelled through ten Eastern and West European cities. Cultural tourism figured also prominently among the activities in the form of, for example, the development and promotion of European cultural itineraries such as the Route of St Jacques de Compostella and the Baroque or Celtic routes in Europe. Partly because of difficulties related to a problem of definition, social tourism attracted little interest. Neverthless some initiatives were taken to assist single parent families, disabled persons and senior citizens. A conference 'Tourism for all in Europe' formed the first step towards European co-operation to improve accessibility to tourism facilities for disabled persons. There was great activity in the sphere of rural tourism and operators in this sector showed great willingness to improve their professionalism and to give a new dimension to this type of tourism. Environmental issues in the development of tourism also played an important role and numerous pilot projects made a contribution to the development and promotion of ecologically friendly forms of tourism.

Conclusions

Despite certain setbacks in the organization of the year (which were related to the short preparation period, staffing problems, limited budget, unequal promotion in the Member States) EYT has provoked interest and mobilization of both institutional and private partners in the tourist industry. The year enabled the Commission to carry out a great deal of activities, especially with regard to the development of new alternative forms of tourism. It was a great opportunity for the Commission to establish contacts with professionals in the tourism sphere both within the EC and outside in particular in the EFTA states and Central and Eastern European countries.[122]

The Commission feels that on the whole the EYT was an important and positive experience.[123] The achievements are considerable. EYT was useful in respect of exchanging information and pooling experience between the Community and those involved in tourism and, indeed, within the Commission itself. Closer links could be established between national and local administrations, trade associations and representatives of the industry and between all these and the Commission. It also facilitated closer co-operation between the various Commission departments (information, environment, social and regional policy). EYT was also an interesting experience in view of the need for a broader framework for the development of new initiatives and exchange of experience between the Member States. For example those responsible for developing rural tourism manifested a desire to improve their professionalism and to make agritourism in Europe more attractive, particularly by establishing European links or entering European competitions which might make their local achievements better known and better rewarded. Cultural tourism projects were most successful and included the promotion of European cultural tourist routes and co-operation between various regions of Europe. The projects financed demonstrated a need for a more effective information policy, for improved co-operation and for Europewide networks for the exchange of experience.

EYT has also shown that transnational co-operation in the sphere of tourism has a multiple effect, especially in relation to so far underdeveloped areas (such as Urban Tourism) or where the need for transfer of experience and expertise is unusually great (such as in the case of co-operation with Central and Eastern Europe). It is, furthermore, important to make operators both within and outside Europe more aware of the richness and diversity of European Tourism. EYT enabled various specific promotion activities that have drawn attention to European Tourism, the nature of the industry and the conditions under which it can be further developed. The Commission feels that the extensive use of the EYT logo could prove beneficial in paving the way for the introduction of the concept of a 'European Tourism Product' in addition to what is already on offer in the regions and in the Member States. The Commission has come to the conclusion that an analysis of the impact of EYT and the importance and diversity of the projects it has generated has highlighted the need for an EC Action Plan to assist tourism supplementing the general measures taken by the EC in the framework of its areas of responsibility or as part of its specific policies. Such plan has meanwhile been presented by the Commission on 24 April 1991 and this will be further discussed in Chapter 5.[124]

4

Actions of Particular Importance for Business and Consumers

THE TRAVEL SPHERE: PACKAGE HOLIDAYS

One of the most crucial EC actions on tourism is the Directive on package holidays. This Directive, laying down common rules on package travel and establishing a minimum level of consumer protection was adopted during the Irish Presidency.[1] As was pointed out above, the Sector of Tourism is an essential part of the Internal Market and it is rapidly gaining in importance in the EC. Tourism has also great potential as a hardcurrency earner for the African, Pacific or Caribbean countries that are associated with the EC in the context of the Lomé Convention. National laws of the Member States on package travel, holidays and tours show great divergences. National practices differ and obstacles to the freedom to provide services as well as distortions of competition result. This Directive aims to eliminate such obstacles by the harmonization of national laws and to achieve a truly common market in services in this sector. Operators, established in a Member State, after the end of 1992 (the deadline for the implementation of the Directive), will be able to offer their services also in other Member States and consumers will enjoy the same conditions abroad as at home as well as a minimum level of protection. These days the package system is an essential part of tourism and it is expected not only that common rules will stimulate greater growth and productivity, but also that tourists from third countries will seek the advantage of guaranteed standards in packages. Currently even within the EC customers are hesitant to purchase packages outside their own Member State.

A package is defined in the Directive as the pre-arranged

combination of at least two of the following (when sold or offered at an inclusive price and when the service covers a period of more than 24 hours or includes overnight accomodation): (1) transport; (2) accommodation; (3) other tourist services accounting for a significant proportion of the package. The information on the package, its price and other conditions of the contract given by the organizer or the retailer must not be misleading (see Article 3). By 'organiser' is understood the person who, other than occasionally, organizes packages and sells or offers them for sale, either directly or via a retailer. Brochures must indicate legibly, comprehensibly and accurately not only the price but also adequate information on matters such as: destination, transport, accommodation (including local tourist classification), meal plan, itinerary, information on passport and visa requirements, health formalities, amount or percentage of price to be paid on account as well as a timetable for payment of the balance, and minimum number of participants required for the package to take place and the deadline for informing the consumer in case of cancellation.

It was felt that the consumer needs to have a record of the terms of the contract.[2] General information in a written or other appropriate form must be provided on passport and visa requirements as well as on the periods for obtaining them and on health formalities. Written information must also be given about times and places of intermediate stops and transport connections, about cabins, berths or sleeper compartments, about a local representative (or at least an emergency telephone number must be provided), whom to contact in case of journeys by minors and about optional insurance. The contract must contain at least the elements listed in an annexe to the Directive: such as: destination, dates, means of transport, and times and points of departure, category or degree of comfort of accommodation, meal plan, minimum number of participants, required for the package, itinerary, excursions, names of organizer, retailer and, where appropriate, insurer, price and taxes etc., payment schedule and methods of payment, special requirements and deadlines for complaints. The consumer must be given a copy of these terms and he may transfer his booking to another person. Contract prices may not be revised unless the contract explicitly provides for the possibility of revision and states how the revised price is going to be calculated and solely to allow for variation in: transport costs, fuel, taxes, landing taxes, (dis)embarkation fees or exchange rates applied to the package. According to the Commission's re-examined proposal, prices could only be revised if the resulting variation was in excess of 2 per cent of the agreed price. The contract price may not be increased within twenty days prior to departure; the Commission's re-examined proposal spoke of thirty days.[3]

The consumer must be notified of significant alterations of terms such as the price, so that he may either withdraw from the contract or accept a rider to it. If he withdraws or if the organizer cancels the package, he is either entitled to a substitute package of the same or higher quality (if the quality is lower he is entitled to a refund of the difference) or to be repaid all sums paid. He is to be compensated by either the organizer or the retailer, whichever the relevant Member State's law requires, for non-performance, except in case of enrolment of less than the minimum required number of participants or because of force majeure.

The organizer must also, after departure, make suitable alternative arrangements at no extra cost to the consumer, in case of significant failure of performance or if the organizer realizes that he will not be able to procure a significant proportion of the services to be provided. Where appropriate, he must compensate the consumer for the difference between services offered and those supplied. Member States must ensure, with regard to the damage for the consumer from failure to perform or improper performance, that the organizer and/or retailer is/are liable unless the defects in the performance of the contract are attributable neither to any fault of theirs nor to that of another supplier of services because of failings attributable to the consumer or to an unconnected party or due to force majeure. Compensation may be limited in accordance with international conventions such as the Warsaw Convention of 1929 on International Carriage by air and the Paris Convention of 1962 on the Liability of Hotelkeepers.

With regard to damage other than personal injury Member States may allow compensation to be limited under the contract provided, however, that such limits are reasonable. Arrangements must be made for the information of consumers and the handling of complaints. In cases of complaints the organizer and/or retailer or his local representative, if there is one, must make prompt efforts to find appropriate solutions. The Commission's reexamined proposal required the availability of public or private bodies where complaints were not resolved amicably. The Directive stipulates that the organizer and/or retailer must also provide sufficient evidence of security for the refund of money paid over and for repatriation in the event of insolvency. Presumably this means his insolvency, but the drafters could have been a little more explicit about exactly whose insolvency they had in mind. The re-examined proposal also asked the Member States to see to it that the organizer and the retailer cover, by way of insurance, their liabilitiy in so far as it is insurable. It furthermore required that in each Member State a guarantee fund be available for payment of claims. The Directive is minimalist and therefore Member States may, if they so wish, adopt more stringent rules.

The importance of this directive cannot easily be underestimated. Every year some 25 million people in the EC make use of package tours, while all package travel affects between 100 and 150 million Community citizens.[4] Between a quarter and a third of holiday-makers complain each year about poor performance of their package travel. The problems are often related to unexpected changes in arrangements after booking and unhelpful tour representatives.[5] At one time tourists returned with tales of unfinished hotels or swimming pools without water. In the seventies it was not uncommon for tourists to find themselves stranded because of bankruptcy of the operator. More recently the problems concern overbooking, transfer to other inferior hotels, change of mode of transport and unhelpful couriers.[6]

The Directive had a long gestation period since the Commission's initial guidelines of 1982 already included proposals for the protection of consumers taking package tours.[7] The Council had adopted the scheme in principle in April 1984.[8] As pointed out above, the latest proposal covered not only holiday trips but all package travellers. Several national governments and the industry had already adopted legislation or self-regulation to protect holiday-makers. In Germany travel contracts come under a 1979 law covering all German contracts. There are, however, no legal obligations in respect of licensing, insurance or guarantee funds. France introduced a law in 1982 which applies to all package travel. In France prices of a package are unalterable except under specific legal conditions. In Spain the travel agent is also considered as a general contractor liable for the proper performance of the whole package and, therefore, a legitimate target for complaints or damages. In the United Kingdom there are no specific laws governing the rights and duties of parties to a travel contract. Much of this business operates under a scheme of self-regulation within the requirements of ordinary contract law. Tour operators must obtain a licence from the CAA (Civil Aviation Authority) covering financial security. ABTA (The Association of British Travel Agents) ensures that customers of tour operators and travel agents are protected against bankruptcy. The operation of the ABTA code of practice is monitored by the Office of Fair Trading. The code (drawn up by the Advertising Standards Authority) covers holiday descriptions, booking conditions, alterations and cancellations of holidays, and price variations. ABTA, furthermore, provides arbitration and conciliation procedures in respect of disputes between a member of the Association and a customer.

The Commission felt that even if there had been improvements of the legal protection of tourists in the Member States, such protection should apply effectively throughout the EC. According to a German study,[9] approximately one third of customers had problems with their package holiday. The figures rose to 37 per cent in the United Kingdom, 32 per cent in former West Germany, 31 per cent in France and 27 per cent in Italy. The Commission was not moved by the argument that the new legislation would raise prices. It believes that there will be no great additional cost for business. Administrative costs of package travel might even be reduced as a result of the Directive which offers a useful arrangement for dealing with deficiences between customers and tour operators or travel agencies.

When the Commission presented its proposal BEUC (the Union of European Consumer Organisations) was of the opinion not only that prices would go up but also that the Directive did not cover enough ground.[10] It was, moreover, worried that if it was left to individual Member States to set up a guarantee fund to safeguard consumers against bankrupt tour operators too many differences would emerge in practice. The Organisation also complained that the Directive was silent on mutual recognition of operator licensinsg and that there was no reference to the responsibility of the travel agent and the general obligations of the tour operator to the traveller. It further felt that the Directive did not spell out the minimum terms of a contract nor that it did anything to harmonize penalties to be enforced in the absence of a contract. BEUC is much impressed by the Spanish law, which allows consumers to insist on all advertised facilities as part of their contract. The Organisation also commented that some problems such as unexpected surcharges or inaccurate brochures have indeed been addressed, but that the Directive would not, as such, promote comparability of brochures. Nevertheless BEUC recognized that the Directive was a positive contribution towards the redressing of the balance between the consumer and the tour operator.

The Commission was also backed by the EP and the ESC. The latter, in its opinion on the draft for this Directive, endorsed the proposal but pointed out that there was a need for common standards not only for package travel but also for the full range of tourist activities as was shown by an examination of the legislation in the Member States, and in particular the legislation governing the organizers and retailers of package travel, the problem of overbooking, the position of the hotelier who is at the end of the chain in any given tour arrangement, and the difficulties caused by the development of the so-called 'bucket-shop' operators.[11]

Other points requiring examination according to the ESC included:

- the establishment of a guarantee fund at EC level, as the operation of such funds in certain Member States is generally considered to be satisfactory;
- the need to dispense justice expeditiously to both consumers and organizers/retailers and indeed to parties to disputes within the travel trade itself.

THE HOTEL AND CATERING SPHERE

Standardized Information on Hotels

First of all there is the recommendation on standardized information on hotels.[12] The Commission made a proposal for a recommendation on standardized information on hotels in January 1986.[13] Even if the measure represents only soft law it is of considerable importance and it is a good example of a measure devised to facilitate tourism. In the Council's resolution of 10 April 1984 on a Community policy on tourism the Commission was specifically asked to present such proposals. It is of great importance to travellers to have standardized information on hotel accommodation using symbols to indicate the facilities available. This is so not only because of linguistic problems but also to take account of other special local features. It is also felt that the national tourist organizations responsible for tourist policy or other competent organizations should be responsible for the implementation of a standardized information system for hotels. Most Member States have a grading system for hotels to indicate the degree of comfort and facilities available.

In addition to such national grading systems there are commercial systems operated by private bodies. However, the existing national and commercial grading systems differ considerably. It has proved difficult to work out a hotel grading system at EC level, given the differing criteria applied, but it is nevertheless felt that it would be desirable to consider the possibility of doing so in the future. The recommendation seeks to overcome language differences and aims to provide the consumer with a simple method of measuring price against facilities provided. It is recommended that Member States ask national tourist bodies or other competent bodies, in collaboration with bodies representing hoteliers, to assume responsibility for implementing the proposed standardized information system for hotels taking into consideration the symbols set out in an annex to the recommendation. This responsibility involves collecting, checking and publishing information on hotels in accordance with the recommendation. It is, furthermore, recommended that Member States encourage the insertion of such standardized information in the official hotel guides, if they exist. Member States should also seek to ensure that the official hotel guide contains certain information. The suggested contents of official hotel guides are the following:

(1) an introduction, explaining how to use the guide, with particular emphasis on the symbols used. This introduction should indicate when the high, shoulder and low season prices apply on a national and/or regional basis, and all useful information in the language of the country in question plus at least two other languages;
(2) lists of hotels giving:
   - their name, address, telephone and telex numbers
   - number of rooms with details of sanitary facilities

- opening period
- maximum price (inclusive of VAT) for a double room in the high season
- distance from airport, railway station and air terminal
- credit and payment cards accepted
- information on languages spoken
- standardized symbols for hotel facilities;

(3) address to which inaccuracies in the information contained in the guide can be reported.

Member States should, furthermore, aim to ensure that the prices of rooms are displayed at hotel entrances and in each room. Member States must send to the Commission each year the official guide(s) published in accordance with the recommendation.

The Commission, finally, was invited to produce an analysis in co-operation with the Member States, of their tourist bodies and/ or representatives of their hotel industries, of existing hotel grading systems and to examine the practical usefulness and the desirability of elaborating an EC-wide grading system for hotels. The Commission has started an analysis of all hotel information systems by undertaking a feasibility study.[14] The first interim report of the study focuses attention on the existing classification systems and explores the attitudes of the various organizations involved in the promotion, administration and operation of the industry. The terms of reference of the report were to examine the existing systems in the Member States, to examine similarities and differences between the various schemes in operation, and to draw up a possible operations scheme for hotel characterization based on the hotel facilities contained in the recommendation. The interim report focuses attention solely on the examination of the existing systems in the Member States and does not endeavour to suggest harmonization formulae for either characterization or classification systems. The final report will embody the contents of the interim report and offer alternatives for hotel characterization-based information systems.

In order to produce the report Horwarth & Horwarth's consultants visited the Member States and a great number of interviews were held with relevant public and private sector organizations. Meetings were held with bodies such as the Commission's Tourism Directorate, the International Hotel Association, the World Tourism Organisation (WTO), National Tourist Boards, National Hotel Associations, National Travel Associations, hoteliers, tour operators, consumer interest groups and private sector grading organizations. The report deals only with classifications in the Member States and characterization will be dealt with in a second phase report. The first interim report basically compares the existing systems and provides a useful summary of the Member States systems, detailed Member State Reports, as well as a section on private classification systems such as those operated by organizations such as the AA in Great Britain, Best Western Hotels – Europe and Michelin. Private systems are implemented in all Member States. Sometimes (e.g. Michelin system) the hotels are included at the discretion of the organization operating the scheme: however, in most cases the scheme is voluntary and is open to hoteliers as a marketing tool.[15]

Private systems are very effective and are geared towards the consumer. Their disadvantage is that the schemes do not cover the entire hotel industry. Therefore national tourism organizations have become involved with hotel classification.

Fire Safety in Hotels

Another interesting measure in the hotel sphere is the recommendation on fire safety in existing hotels.[16] Since rules on fire safety in all hotels did not exist in all Member States some EC action was required. Even where they did exist the provisions were not complete, were contained in several different texts and were not always fully observed.

These days more and more people need to stay in hotels in other Member States than their own and they are entitled to adequate protection. It was, furthermore, considered that the safety of guests should be compatible with that of staff at work. The objective of the Council recommendation was to define a minimum standard of fire safety for all hotels and it was felt that their conformity with such minimum standard was essential for their continuing operation and that it was advisable to subject hotels to periodic inspections. It was also felt that although for economic, technical and architectural reasons it would take some time to fully introduce fire precautions in hotels, there should be reasonable time limits for the objective in question to be achieved. Fire precautions in hotels based on a minimum standard of safety should, furthermore, help to prepare and promote harmonization work in progress elsewhere. It was considered important to promote the circulation and dissemination of information regarding measures adopted at national level to protect hotels against the risks of fire and the Commission was called upon to play an essential role in the provision and dissemination of such information. It was, therefore, recommended to the Member States to take all appropriate measures in so far as the existing laws are not already sufficient to meet the requirements of the recommendation to ensure that fire precautions in the existing hotels are subject to the provisions based on the principles of the recommendation.

The aims and means of the recommendation are as follows. The introduction of fire precautions is intended to reduce the risk of fire breaking out, to prevent the spread of flames and smoke, to ensure that all occupants can be safely evacuated and to enable the emergency services to take action. To meet these objectives, precautions must be taken within the establishment so that:

- safe escape routes are available, are clearly indicated and remain accessible and unobstructed;
- the building's structural stability in the event of fire is guaranteed at least for as long as it is needed for the occupants to evacuate the building safely;
- the presence or use of higly inflammable materials in wall, ceiling or floor coverings and interior decorations is carefully limited;
- all technical equipment and appliances operate safely;
- appropriate systems are installed and maintained in proper working order for alerting occupants;
- safety instructions and a plan of the premises with an indication of the escape routes are displayed in each room normally occupied by guests or staff;
- emergency fire fighting equipment such as extinguishers is provided and maintained in proper working order;
- the staff is given suitable instruction and training.

When applying these principles to the existing commercially run establishments which occupy all or part of a building and which under the name of hotel, boarding house, inn, tavern, motel or other equivalent designation can offer accommodation to at least twenty temporary paying guests, Member States should take into account a number of technical guidelines set out in a detailed annex to the recommendation. For example, escape routes must be arranged and located in such a way as to lead independently into the street or into an open space large enough to allow people to move away from the building and to enable persons to evacuate the premises quickly and safely. Doors, staircases, exits and routes thereto must be indicated by standard safety signs visible day and night.

Other guidelines on escape routes are concerned with the direction of the opening of doors and the obstruction of escape routes. For example, doors located on escape routes must, as far as possible, be capable of opening in the intended direction of evacuation. Final exit doors of an escape route must be capable of being opened easily from the inside by a person escaping from the hotel, etc.

There are also guidelines on construction features. For example, the construction features must be such that the fire resistance of the load-bearing components is adequate to ensure the structural stability of the whole for a sufficient length of time in the event of fire. There are detailed guidelines on matters such as building structures, floors, staircase enclosures (staircases with more than two levels above the ground must be enclosed) and partitions. Coverings and decorations are also covered in the guidelines. Interior coverings and decorations must be such as not to constitute a particular hazard by contributing to fire spread and smoke production. There is a minimum safety standard required for interior coverings and decorations in the escape routes.

Other guidelines deal with electric lighting (e.g. the principal lighting system must be an electric one and all hotel establishments must have a suitable emergency lighting system, which is capable to enable all occupants to be evacuated if the principal system fails) heating and ventilation systems, fire-fighting, alarm and alerting equipment. In respect of the latter hotel staff must be required to participate at least twice a year in instruction and training sessions involving the operation of the emergency fire-fighting equipment and the alerting and alarm system and in evacuation exercises. Furthermore, in the entrance halls of the hotel, precise instructions must be prominently posted on action to be taken by the staff and the residents in the event of fire.

The guidelines also cover other safety instructions, such as prominently posted and precise instructions in each bedroom indicating the action to be taken in the event of fire. These instructions must be posted also in appropriate foreign languages depending on the origin of the hotel's usual guests and the instructions must be accompanied by a simplified floor plan showing schematically the location of the room in relation to escape routes, staircases and or exits.

Member States may use different or more stringent measures than those specified in the guidelines, but these must achieve an equivalent result. In particular, the alternative solution must ensure the overall minimum safety standard which the provisions of the guidelines are designed to establish. It is, furthermore, recommended that Member States subject hotels to periodic inspection of their conformity with the national provisions based on the principles of the recommendation. They finally should inform the Commission of all national measures designed to ensure that hotels meet the above-mentioned requirements and of the measures they intend to take within the five years following the adoption of the recommendation. The European Parliament has invited the Commission to make a proposal for a regulation on the protection of establishments offering accommodation, campsites and discotheques against fire risks further to the recommendation of 23 December 1986.[17] The Parliament is of the opinion that the responsibility for complying with more stringent safety requirements should rest with local authorities.

5

Latest EC Action Plan to Assist Tourism

The latest thinking is that the EC should implement a coherent plan to supplement the abovementioned initiatives already taken under common policies or specific programmes.[1] Thus all aspects of tourism will be covered to achieve an all-round improvement in the quality and competitiveness of tourism facilities and services in the EC. The measures of the action plan, which was presented by the Commission on 24 April 1991, have as their objective to assist tourist activities to adjust to the changes in the business environment resulting from the completion of the Internal Market and economic and monetary union and to the shift in demand towards diversification and better quality, in the framework of growing international competition. Most measures follow on from what has already been done but there are some quite new initiatives as well, such as the development of certain transnational schemes. Small scale promotional activities will gain a new dimension through the image of the EC as a single market.

The Action plan will focus attention on two main priorities: (1) the strengthening of the horizontal approach to tourism both in national and EC policies; (2) support for specific measures to assist tourism in the EC.

STRENGTHENING OF THE HORIZONTAL APPROACH

There is a need to achieve greater consistency between the various measures taken to assist tourism. It is felt, therefore, that the first objective should be to gain a more accurate picture of the present situation and the development problems faced in all areas of the tourist industry.

Horizontal action will be taken in five main areas:

(a) improving the knowledge of the tourist industry;
(b) co-ordination of EC and national policies;
(c) organizing consultation with the tourism industry;
(d) improved staggering of holidays and dispersion of tourism;
(e) improved protection for the tourist as consumer.

Improving Knowledge of the Tourist Industry

As was seen in Chapter 2, improving knowledge of the tourist industry and the changes taking place within it is a prerequisite for improvement of Community action in this field.

Statistics

The Council has meanwhile taken a Decision on 17 December 1990 on the implementation of a two-year programme for developing EC tourism statistics and it did so in response to requests from the Member States and the industry itself.[2] The programme aims to define and introduce an EC framework of reference for tourism statistics by bringing together concepts and methods used in the Member States.

Various stages are planned:

- analysis and evaluation of user requirements as regards tourism statistics;
- analysis of existing national systems;
- preparation of an EC methodological framework;
- collection and dissemination of the existing data on tourism.

The European Parliament has welcomed the Council decision but has pointed out that the resources allocated must be sufficient to permit the necessary surveys to be properly completed and it has requested the Commission to make available as wide a selection as possible of statistics on a regional basis.[3]

The Commission, in co-operation with the tourism industry and government departments, is studying ways of disseminating information to users. A complementary data processing system is also to be devised and, as pointed out in Chapter 2, the setting up of a documentation and information centre in this field is being studied.

Studies

A programme of forward planning and discussions will provide information for identifying trends concerning the expansion of tourism activities. The aim of the programme is to improve knowledge of tourism demand from inside and outside Europe, so as to examine the conditions for adjusting tourism supply to changes in demand, and to initiate feasibility studies on the development of adjustment strategies. The result of the studies will be published as widely as possible.

Co-ordination of Community and National Policies

It is seen as important that EC firms adjust to the rapidly changing business and social environment. To ensure that greater account is taken of tourism in other policies the Commission will strengthen existing co-operation between the departments concerned. Co-ordination of EC policies must be complemented by improved co-ordination at EC level of national policies to assist tourism. Therefore the Commission will strengthen co-operation with the Member States, within the advisory Committee on tourism[4] through more frequent and regular meetings. The Commission will furthermore make sure that decisions regarding the implementation of EC policy are better communicated. An initial information document on EC policies and measures affecting tourism, from the point of view of the completion of the Internal Market, has already been drawn up.[5]

Consultation with the Industry

Consultation should also take place with the trade associations in the tourist industry. Several representatives of the industry are already members of the Committee on Commerce and Distribution. Others participate in the regular meetings on the co-operative, mutual and non-profit sector. The Commission is not thinking of setting up an additional structure to these channels. However, tourist trade associations can be consulted at the meetings of the Advisory Committee, to which their representatives and officers of European tourism bodies and representatives of the Consumer Consultative Committee would be invited to discuss specific matters.

Improved Staggering of Holidays

The staggering of holidays, which was discussed in Chapter 2, is a matter of growing concern both for the tourist authorities and the tourist industry.

The excessive concentration in particular areas at particular times of the year has serious consequences such as transport delays, overbooked accommodation and transport services, overcharging, deterioration of services, environmental deterioration, etc.[6] The staggering of holidays is largely a transnational problem and the Commission is, of course, well placed to play a major role in encouraging and co-ordinating national or regional measures and initiatives to assist the spreading of holidays and the dispersion of tourism.

EC action will be threefold:

(1) follow-up to the 1986 Resolution and the 1991 conference on the staggering of holidays:[7] The Commission will analyse both the results of a survey of the Member States and the conclusions of a conference on the geographical and seasonal distribution of tourism. An informal working party will be set up to analyse the results of these two initiatives and, in co-operation with the Member States, to examine areas where co-ordinated measures could be taken;

(2) experimental cooperation procedure: the Commission will have to organize meetings to prepare for possible consultations between the various parties in decisions governing holiday periods such as educational authorities, employers and workers, consumers and representatives from the various branches of the tourist industry;

(3) pilot schemes: the Commission will participate in a number of pilot schemes testing new ideas within one Member State, or the transfer of best practice between Member States and it will co-ordinate the publication and distribution of information on such pilot schemes.

Protection of Tourists

Several aspects of protection of tourists have been discussed in Chapters 2 and 4. However, initiatives so far provide only partial protection to tourists. It is felt that the development of tourist activities should be considered from the point of view of both supply and demand. The tourist should be protected as the purchaser of both services and goods. Another problem is that the degree of protection of tourists, for a number of tourism activities, varies from Member State to Member State. This is in particular the case in respect of thc independent traveller who has not taken a package holiday. Coherent measures that will guarantee tourists adequate protection are indeed required.

The European Parliament has considered this matter on several occasions and is studying a report on 'Tourism and the Consumer'.[8] The Commission's guidelines with regard to improved information and protection of tourists are concerned with measures such as:

- the drafting of a proposal for filling major gaps in information for tourists;
- the drafting of a proposal concerning cross-border property transactions (time-sharing);
- a study on the possibilities for complaints by tourists as individual consumers under a speedy, simple and inexpensive procedure.

Tourist assistance

Council Directive 84/641 amends Directive 73/239 and thereby extends the latter to provide insurance cover in the form of tourist assistance.

The first Council Directive 73/239 on the co-ordination of laws, regulations and administrative provisions relating to the taking-up and pursuit of the business of direct insurance other than life insurance, as amended by Directive 76/580, eliminated certain differences between the laws of the Member States in order to facilitate the taking-up and the pursuit of the above business.[9] According to Article 1, paragraph 2 of Directive 84/641 this activity covers assistance to persons who get into difficulties while travelling, while away from home or while away from their permanent residence. It consists in undertaking, against the prior payment of a premium, to make aid immediately available to the beneficiary under an assistance contract when that person is in difficulties following the occurrence of a chance event, in the cases and under the conditions set out in the contract. The aid may consist in the provision of benefits in cash or in kind, but assistance activity does not cover servicing, maintenance, after sales service or the mere indication or provision of aid as an intermediary. In more concrete terms the Directive is about assistance activity to motorists such as on-the-spot breakdown service and conveyance of the vehicle to the nearest or the most appropriate location for repair.

According to Article 3 the accident or breakdown must have occurred in the territory of the Member State of the undertaking providing cover. No such condition, however, applies to the situation where the latter is a body of which the beneficiary is a member and the breakdown assistance, etc. is provided simply on presentation of a membership card, without any additional premium being paid, by a similar body in the country concerned on the basis of a reciprocal agreement. Neither is the provision of such assistance in Ireland and in the United Kingdom by a single body operating in both countries precluded. According to Article 3, the Directive does not apply to undertakings which fulfil certain conditions.

The preamble of the Directive also stresses that the sole fact of providing certain forms of assistance on the occasion of an accident or breakdown involving a road vehicle normally occurring in the territory of the Member State of the undertaking providing cover, is not a reason for any person or undertaking that is not an insurance undertaking to be subject to the arrangements of the first Directive. It is, furthermore, pointed out that the purpose of the inclusion, for reasons of supervision, of assistance operations in the scope of the first Directive is not to affect the fiscal rules applicable to them. The drafters of the measure also felt that provision ought to be made for certain relaxations to the condition that the accident or breakdown must occur in the territory of the Member State of the undertaking providing cover in order to take into account either the existence of reciprocal agreements or of certain specific circumstances relating to the geographical situation or to the structure of the organizations concerned, or to the very limited economic importance of the operations referred to.

SUPPORT FOR SPECIFIC MEASURES

It is felt that the horizontal approach alone, important as it is in an area such as tourism, is not sufficient since some problems, as was seen above, evidently require specific action at EC level.

The EC, as has been pointed out above, is already heavily committed on the side of the supply of tourism through the structural funds and through specific training programmes. These actions involve investment in either accommodation, infrastructure or human resources. Such actions are mostly limited to areas that are eligible for regional development. Actions that are not covered across the EC include better transparency in the market, innovation, improved quality, and research into a better balance between supply and demand. It is in this area that the specific measures envisaged are complementary to actions already organized by the EC. When defining these measures, added value to a Community action was the main criterion for selection. The measures have largely been identified by synergy between the different (public or private) operators and the snowball effect of an impetus at EC level. The latest action programme points out that only the EC can instigate co-operative actions or joint ventures that go beyond the regional or national framework. This also goes for transferring experience or implementing best practices through competitions or publications.[10]

Diversification of Joint Activities in the Medium Term and Improvement of Quality

EC action to assist rural tourism business

As was pointed out in Chapter 2 (p. 24), the Commission has adopted a communication on an action programme (1991–4) in favour of rural tourism business.[11] The programme, in line with the objectives of the European Year of Tourism, aims to support diversification, improvements to quality and promotion of rural tourism products. It is essential, *inter alia* given increasing competition in the form of tourist products outside Europe, that new quality products are provided. Rural tourism is indeed a natural alternative to mass tourism and Europe's rural environment has great potential which should be promoted such as scenery, authenticity, local cultures, architectural heritage, and personal contacts between local inhabitants and tourists. The forms and concepts of rural tourism differ from Member State to Member State. It is therefore felt that the notion of rural tourism products must be broadened so as to include more than mere agritourism (farm-based tourism) to which it is often linked. It is also stressed in the latest action plan that rural tourism involves all forms of tourism in a rural environment.

Rural tourism measures will be implemented in conjunction with operators in the industry where necessary and will focus on the following aims:

- to help define rural tourism products by improving information on demand for such products and enhancing the transparency of supply and by harmonizing information on all components of rural tourism products (system of appropriate symbols);
- to assist in the creation and development of rural tourism products by improving information on and access to EC aid schemes for rural tourism; by assisting local authorities in respect of rural tourism; by promoting co-operation between those involved locally; by measures to improve the management of rural tourism activities through support for training measures, exchanges and the setting up of networks;
- to promote access to the market in rural tourism products by better customer information (use of a system of European symbols) by encouraging improvements in the quality of rural tourism products; by promotion aimed at national and local officials; by support for the marketing of rural tourism products at EC level and by support for the creation of a European network for the distribution of rural tourism products.

Action with regard to cultural tourism

European Tourism has to deal with two challenges. It has to diversify to be able to meet continually growing demand and it has to absorb an increase in activities without destroying the European cultural heritage. In Chapter 2 the importance of cultural tourism has been stressed: it is an important part of tourist activity in the EC and it attracts increasing numbers of tourists both from inside and outside the Community. It has already been pointed out that the various forms of cultural tourism can contribute towards the staggering of flows of tourists and to the promotion of new destinations. Tourism and cultural tourism also may assist increasing mutual understanding and recognition of the various aspects of European culture. The projects in cultural tourism emanating from the European Year of Tourism have prepared the ground for longer term action by the EC.[12]

The actions include:

- research and exchange of information with regard to visitor management techniques: several research centres, universities and expert bodies are engaged in developing techniques, procedures and solutions for problems concerning the connection between exploitation and conservation. According to the latest action plan a European information system capable of ensuring the dissemination of information on this topic would be an appropriate response to the need for information, exchange of experience and comparison of results which has been voiced by those involved in tourism and cultural institutions in all Member States. Networking will permit members to participate actively in the circulation and continuous updating of information;
- a European prize for the best Cultural Tourism products: the Commission will support the launching of such a prize which is to be organized and managed by an outside body. It is hoped that the catalogue of the cultural tourism covered by the competition could be a first trial for the production of a European guide to cultural tourism.
- New European cultural itineraries: as was seen in Chapter 3 (p. 60), EC support was given to several pan-European projects for the creation of European cultural itineraries for tourists. The objective is to give priority to continuing this action in order to encourage co-operation between Member States and other European countries such as EFTA countries and Eastern European ones to develop existing routes and encourage the creation of new ones. It is also felt that the creation of cultural products on a European scale can assist in meeting demand from outside for European products. Existing European cultural routes will also be supported if they have a tourism dimension. The programme will be organized by a project selection committee consisting of representatives of the Commission, the Council of Europe, the Member States and European organizations in this field. The publication at European level of the various cultural routes, in

the form of guides or theme-based maps, is seen as one of the most effective ways of supporting the advertising campaign carried out by the promoters of these routes;
- actions in co-operation with museums – 'Tourmuse' the pan-European museum competition supported under the European Year of Tourism: the objective of this action is to promote, through competition, a better provision for tourism in museums. Museums are invited to propose a complete package in association with a tourism partner (tour operator, tourist office, local authority, etc.).

The Commission will support the regular publication of the results of this extremely interesting and important competition. In this way it will assist in the dissemination of information on new initiatives for better understanding and co-operation between culture and tourism circles.

According to the action plan there is scope for improvement in the way visitors are received in museums in Europe. On the whole, the provision of the information material, comprehensive labelling and guided visits are quite adequate. It is obvious though that such services can be pointless if the documentation, etc. is provided only in the language of the country in question. Language barriers should be removed for the benefit of both visitors from inside and those from outside Europe. The EC would like to see improvement in the facilities (by Member States, cultural authorities and tourism and culture professionals) for foreign visitors such as information material in several languages, including minority languages at the major centres of cultural tourism in Europe.

Eco-tourism

As was pointed out in Chapter 3 (p. 61) there is increasing concern that tourism should develop in harmony with the environment. Overcrowding, over-exploitation and depletion of resources have caused considerable environmental deterioration. The ESC, in particular, has suggested a new approach.[13] As was pointed out above, the European Commission also sees to it that Member States take into consideration the environmental impact of investment projects proposed for EC finance. In talks with the Member States on regional development programmes for which EC funding is being sought under the structural funds, the Commission has already brought its influence to bear in order to achieve a better balance between the development of tourism and the protection of the environment. It is felt that, to promote environmentally friendly forms of tourism, further measures should be envisaged to strengthen the links between tourism and the environment.[14]

The EC will support the following specific action:

- encouraging the drawing up of inventories of tourism resources in the Member States. Such inventories would be compiled by the Member States as instruments in the drafting of regional and tourism development programmes. There is also the idea of the setting up of a network of regions experiencing the same type of problems, such as coastal areas, mountainous regions, since an assessment of the impact of the development of tourism in such regions could prove useful;
- the awarding of an EC environment prize could also be useful in that it would further encourage the various sectors of the tourist industry to widen their professional experience. It would also give rise to an information network on ecologically valid professional experience in various sectors of the tourist industry, such as hotels, restaurants and the transport sector. This type of scheme has proved very successful at national level. It is, furthermore, felt that the experience gained in the course of the Blue Flag Campaign should be taken into consideration. This Campaign was launched in 1987, the European Year of the Environment. The Commission financially supported this campaign in the framework of its action to raise awareness of the environmental problems among citizens of the EC. The Commission's involvement in this campaign is also justified in view of the EC Directive on the quality of bathing water,[15] which lays down a number of values corresponding to various microbiological and physico-chemical parameters. Other parameters considered as indicators of pollution, such as pesticides, heavy metals, nitrates and phosphates may also be taken into account.

Directive 76/160 lays down two categories of values: imperative values which Member States must respect and (stricter) guide values which Member States must try to achieve. Member States were given until December 1985 to set values which bathing waters had to meet, and which at least equal the imperative values. Member States must report to the Commission at regular intervals on the state of their bathing waters and the Commission publishes its information in an annual report. The Commission is improving the data transmission and presentation in order to provide the public with more uniform and comparable information on the quality of bathing water in the community. Blue Flags are awarded on the basis of twenty-seven criteria which fall into three categories: water quality, beach quality and information and education.

The first criterion refers specifically to the bathing water Directive and is formulated as follows: compliance with the microbiological parameters of the EC bathing water Directive or national/regional legislation, whichever is stricter. There is some risk of confusion and misunderstanding because the values and parameters applied in the context of the Directive vary from country to country, and this diversity is reflected in the criteria used for the blue flag. Holiday-makers, nevertheless, have come to see the blue flag as a quality label especially for water quality. The Commission feels that such a label should only be given to beaches where, in addition to compliance with the specific Blue Flag criteria for clean beaches, information and education, the bathing water Directive is applied in an exemplary way. In other words all the mandatory parameters should be taken into account and where guide values as well as imperative values are given, the water quality should comply with the guide value. The Commission still considers the Blue Flag campaign as experimental and has asked the initiator of the campaign and owner of the blue flag logo, the Foundation for Environmental Education in Europe (FEEE), and the National Blue Flag organisers to present it as such to the general public. Blue flags for beaches and marinas were awarded in 1990 to 697 beaches and 160 marinas in Europe.[16] The Commission's continued commitment to the blue flag will depend on general application of strict and uniform criteria for bathing water quality. Meanwhile the success of the Blue Flag Campaign is valuable to raise awareness in the field of the environment and it is felt that the EC should take this experience into consideration. The Commission not only lends financial support to this campaign but is also involved in drawing up the criteria for making the awards, and is represented on the European Jury.[17]

Another specific action the EC will support is the drawing up of a code of behaviour for tourists. The aim of such a code, based on schemes emanating from the European Year of Tourism, would be to limit the various schemes being implemented in this field in order to produce a single message addressed to all tourists. If necessary such a document could be the subject of a Council recommendation. It is felt that the drawing up of a practical guide aimed at the industry, which will contain recommendations that may make it easier to take environmental factors into account when devising tourism products and facilities would benefit the development of Eco-tourism.

Another action concerns the exchange of experience in visitor management. Thus best practices in this field at EC level will be identified and made available to local authorities as a recommended basis for improving visitor management during busy periods. Finally there is the action of support for pilot projects in Eco-tourism. Continuing from the experience gained in the context of the European Year of Tourism the EC will financially support pilot projects or actions that provide a useful incentive in respect of the development of initiatives in environmental tourism.

Action to improve the quality of tourism through vocational training

As the explanatory memorandum to the EC's action plan points out, expanding tourism in the EC and Europe, and thus maintaining Europe as the leading world tourist destination, depends on a supply of quality products and services capable of meeting the increasing demands of consumers of tourism products. This, in turn, depends on the human resources available and their level of training. Some aspects of vocational training have already been dealt with in Chapter 2 (see p. 33). Tourism and all the firms in this industry are well placed to benefit from the entire range of EC measures designed to foster training in Europe. However, because of some specific factors, by which tourism is characterized, such as seasonality and the fact that many firms are quite small, the number of companies participating in the programmes is disproportionate to the importance of the sector and the magnitude of its training requirements. Occupational profiles in the industry are not always clearly defined, particularly because widely differing occupations are often found alongside each other. Therefore there are problems in respect of the short-term management of human resources, both in relation to management training and the skills of workers. For the same reason it is difficult to identify the industry's long-term training needs.

The Commission will implement the following types of measures.

Identifying occupational profiles: Since the absence of well-defined occupational profiles is an obstacle to the implementation of vocational training schemes in the tourist industry, the setting up of the necessary machinery to identify and adapt the occupational profiles concerned is one of the prime objectives of measures to foster vocational training in this sector;

Dialogues within the industry: There is a move towards closer sectoral dialogue, which the Commission has already started to put into effect in the case of the hotel and restaurant industry. It is the intention to identify needs at the various levels, to plot occupational profiles, define training programmes in respect of each profile etc. It is felt, furthermore, that this process should continue in order to take account of the other sectors which involve tourism activity.

Ensuring greater involvement by firms in the tourist sector in EC training programmes and measures: The EC's programmes and measures designed to foster vocational training in Europe, although designed to deal with specific problems, are general in nature and are not intended mainly or exclusively for individual sectors within the tourism industry. It is felt that the industry should be subjected to an effective awareness campaign involving brochures, meetings with agencies responsible for the implementation of the programmes at national level, and information aimed specifically at the business interests and unions concerned.

Many tourist and hotel schools have always produced highly qualified personnel. However a great deal of SME's in the tourist and hotel trade, the firms that form the backbone of the industry, fail to take advantage of the growth potential offered by vocational training. Therefore the Centre for the Development of Vocational Training (CEDEFOP) is promoting an experimental project of continuing training for the managers of small tourist and hotel enterprises.[18] The scheme is directed particularly at tourist areas geographically remote from the centres for the provision of vocational training. It will thus be experimenting with multimedia distance training methods. Given the fact that the tourist industry has traditionally employed a multitude of migrant workers and seasonal workers it is clear that the problem of the equivalence of vocational qualifications is even more urgent in this sector than in others and needs to be solved urgently. CEDEFOP has already carried out a preliminary comparison of second level qualifications (skilled workers) in the HORECA sector, and it has now initiated a scheme for the production of a Community Register of job profiles in the tourist/hotel industry. The first step is to analyse the structure of employment in the tourist and hotel industry and the vocational skills needed there. Then job profiles in a number of occupations within the Member States must be compared. The Register should compare job contents and vocational skills in tourist and hotel occupations. This resource could also serve as a tool for the process of realising the recognition of job qualifications which is so crucial to the functioning of the Internal Market.

The work being done by the Commission with the technical assistance of the Centre for the Development of Vocational Training to implement Council Decision 85/368/EEC of 16 July 1985[19] on the comparability of vocational training qualifications between the Member States is at an advanced stage.[20] The Commission has published comparative tables of qualifications in respect of occupations at skilled worker level in a number of industries including the hotel and catering industry.[21] The Commission has also devised the model for the information sheet that is intended to enable migrant workers in these occupations to take advantage of the comparabilities that have been established and make their skills better known.[22] The communication on comparability of vocational training qualifications in respect of the hotel and catering industry covers the following occupations: receptionist, porter, storeperson, floor supervisor, waiter/waitress, barman/maid, chef and wine waiter/waitress.

Support for pilot international co-operation schemes: This is concerned with the exploration of new fields with a view to devising community training programmes and identifying new ways of responding to training requirements occurring because of changes in the supply of tourism products, such as rural and cultural tourism, Eco-tourism and the social and youth aspect. Such action will benefit from experience gained in other programmes such as FORCE, PETRA, EUROFORM which provided a great deal of answers to the problems of initial and continuing vocational training. FORCE is concerned with the development of continuing vocational training in the EC (1990–3);[23] PETRA is a community action programme for the vocational training of young people and their preparation for adult working life;[24] EUROFORM is concerned with the improvement of employment opportunities and new qualifications through vocational training and employment.[25]

As pointed out in Chapter 2 transnational co-operation between agencies specialising in training in the field of tourism will also be encouraged.

Access for a greater number of people

It is obvious that tourism has a crucial role to play in the realization of a People's Europe because of the many contacts and exchanges it creates and since it fosters closer mutual awareness among different nations and cultures.However, since 40 per cent of Europeans do not yet travel on holiday, EC action, as pointed out in Chapter 2, will be directed at certain less advantaged categories of the population. Young people are also targeted: even though they travel more than their parents did, they are confronted with special problems.

The EC envisages the following measures.

General measures to improve access for the less well off: Social tourism is a relatively vague concept. It covers various aspects and it differs from Member State to Member State. For some the aim of social tourism is to provide citizens on low incomes with a means of going on holiday. For others the concept includes other categories of the population that, for various reasons, cannot travel easily, such as the elderly, handicapped people, the young or single parent families. For the EC social tourism amounts to a means of enabling people to take a holiday. The explanatory memorandum to the EC action plan stresses that social tourism enables 'Tourism for all' and that currently nearly one European in two never travels on holiday. Social tourism has been strongly influenced by changes in tourism in general. There has been great diversification in the range of products on offer as well as easier access by most people to such products and we have seen a profound change in tourist habits.

Measures to improve operating conditions of the supply of social tourism: The objective here is to reorganize facilities by supporting linkage between the various owners, so that they can take measures together. This will involve networking and grading of social tourism facilities. The aim is also integration of facilities combining the group tourism structures of different countries. For example some Members of BITS (International Bureau of Social Tourism) have recently set up a company with the aim of creating a network of tourist villages ('Eurovillages').[26] So the customer base will be broadened by diversifying supply throughout the EC.

Measures to assist diversification of demand: Here the aim is to support social tourism bodies to determine specific measures to assist their customers. This may involve the study and application of seasonal tariffs that will facilitate the staggering of holidays, or of the reasons why certain groups take their holidays at particular times of the year. In this context the extension of the French and Swiss 'cheques vacances' experiment (holiday vouchers) will be discussed.

Handicapped Tourists

Pilot schemes to aid handicapped tourists are aimed to ensure that the handicapped can travel. There are 50 million of them in the Community. The EC aims to facilitate access to tourism by the handicapped and others such as the elderly and parents with very young children.

Assistance will be given to two initiatives:

- the production of a European Guide on 'accessible Europe'. The guide, to be produced in co-operation with national tourist offices, will comprise details of travel opportunities, accommodation and other information for handicapped tourists;
- the preparation of a European brochure giving advice on the provision of tourist facilities. This instrument is aimed at developers and architects and will provide information to ensure that tourist facilities and accommodation are designed with an eye to accessibility. This tool could be useful for hotel owners and builders engaged in renovation.

Under the auspices of the EYT the Commission co-financed a pan-European Conference entitled 'Tourism for All in Europe', held at Gatwick in March 1991.[27] On the basis of the recommendations of this Conference the EC will seek to facilitate access.

Older Tourists

The number of older people increases and this category of tourists tends to take holidays outside peak periods. EC action in respect of this group will involve encouraging the relevant organizations to reflect on this category's specific problems and to assist the implementation of measures required to facilitate tourism for the older traveller. In particular support will be given to the creation of a European card granting special advantages to older tourists.

A pilot programme for elderly people organized during the EYT is a good illustration of a specially organized product on offer to meet the needs of elderly people for travel and constructive recreation. This consisted of six themed trips in the low season. The themes included artistic creativity, culture, European history, health, the arts and European traditions and were spread among weekly vacations in comfortable resorts in France, Spain, Greece and Italy from June until November.[28] The evaluation of this project will create the basis for an extension of aids on offer on a long term basis.

Youth Tourism

One of the objectives of the European Year of Tourism was the promotion among young people of the cultures and lifestyles of other Member States. Youth tourism is one of the best ways of organizing exchanges and forming links. The explanatory memorandum to the action plan points out that there are 51 million young people between 15 and 26 years of age in the EC (i.e. 16 per cent of the population). The travel industry may not always be taken in by poor young travellers, but tourism needs the young who are the affluent travellers of the future and who also are becoming increasingly interested in working in tourism.

The EC will carry out specific measures in order to facilitate travel and tourism for young people in co-operation with the competent bodies. The EC will give its support to the organization of a European youth forum to include the principal youth travel organizations in order to facilitate youth travel. Initially the forum could focus attention on the following:

- increase the special benefits available to young people in respect of travel and holidays and make them transferable. The aim is to provide a single permit (youth card) valid throughout the EC for

the widest possible range of facilities in respect of travel and tourism, including in the cultural sphere;
- dissemination of information to young people on job opportunities in tourism. Such information will improve knowledge of the industry and thus will draw into the tourist trade the extra skills it needs.

Transnational measures

The EYT has demonstrated the importance of co-operation between towns, regions and Member States. The Year has allowed the Commission and operators to establish and maintain a great number of contacts with professionals in the tourist sector both within and outside the EC, which form an excellent basis for new co-operation. Some of the competitions initiated during EYT have highlighted the wide range of existing projects and experience, and have helped to focus efforts and motivate innovative or evolving measures which are relevant to medium-term action. Most of these initiatives are pilot schemes designed for subsequent incorporation into the existing EC programmes. One of these, PHARE, is concerned with assistance for economic restructuring of Poland and Hungary.[29]

It is felt that such projects have the following advantages:

- they enable the expansion of activities relating to specific subjects of demonstrated feasibility;
- they facilitate close contact between the Commission and the industry;
- they serve as models and as a solid basis for subsequent development of general programmes.

The EC will support the following:

- the promotion of transnational co-operation; this involves support for the expansion of transnational tourism co-operation programmes launched in the context of EYT;
- development of commercial links with countries in Central and Eastern Europe. The transfer of know-how is one of the most important elements of co-operation with these countries. One is thinking in particular of the extension of the experience of training trainers for the management of tourist sites initiated in Poland and Hungary;

– the implementation of new forms of tourism and technical co-operation between towns.

In this context it is also necessary to think of the development of urban tourism.[30]

Promotion of European Tourism on International Markets

As the explanatory memorandum to the action plan points out, Europe as a whole, as a tourist destination, is steadily losing world market share. New competitors are emerging whose activities have been facilitated by developments in air transport. It is therefore felt that, to react to this, tourist destinations in the Community must intensify their promotional activities on the world market. In 1986 as many as one third of foreign destinations visited by the Americans were within the EC. In that year expenditure by the American visitors accounted for 8 per cent of the EC's tourist receipts of $55 billion, an impressive figure when compared with the USA's $13 billion in receipts from foreign visitors.[31] The EC, therefore, decided in that year to join the European Travel Commission (ETC) in its efforts to remind the American public of what Europe has to offer to the culture-conscious, travel-oriented Americans. It involved, *inter alia*, a specific EC advertising campaign to promote twelve European destinations in major US daily newspapers.

At present, after the Gulf War with its disastrous consequences for tourism and American tourism in Europe, in particular, there is even more reason to step up efforts to promote European tourism on the world market. The EC feels that the objective of promoting European tourism on international markets can be achieved in two ways:

(a) to increase the capacity for EC firms to sell their products on third country markets, either directly or via agreements with foreign firms. Third country firms have penetrated the EC market significantly. EC Firms must enjoy operating conditions in third countries which are comparable to those obtaining in the EC. Existing unwarranted barriers should disappear. The adoption in multinational trade negotiations of the concept of national treatment would enable services to be provided in cases where national regulations reserve certain activities for nationals or national firms. The structure of the industry also needs to be reinforced. With a few exceptions, the majority of travel agencies and tour operators in the EC are small firms for whom it is difficult to penetrate the markets of third countries;

(b) to increase the promotion of European Tourism in third countries. Measures to promote European Tourism in the USA and Canada have been taken for a number of years by the Commission in co-operation with the European Tourism Commission, which groups together the national tourist organizations of 24 European Countries.[32] The measures took the form of publicity campaigns in newspapers and magazines. More recent measures have also included Latin Amcrica. There is a need, however, for stepping up these and other efforts such as those made during the EYT (including projects related to the discovery of the New World, and the Channel Tunnel).

The new image of Europe with its nearly completed single market and the prospect of economic and monetary union is bound to facilitate marketing in third countries. The gradual emergence of Central and Eastern Europe on the tourist market can only help to make Europe more attractive as a holiday destination. The Commission is planning to conduct a volume campaign addressed at a large population segment, particularly in the USA and Japan, using both television and the Press.

An initial campaign will be built on the 1992 concept which is already well known in these countries. Other campaigns could be carried out by way of television programmes produced in connection with EYT, such as the CIRCOM regional series of programmes[33] or the 'Europuzzle' – a televised competition in which viewers are invited to identify European landmarks presented in a puzzle while questions are asked about the locations shown. Prizes consist of 200 trips to European destinations and include the 'Euro Domino Rail Pass' a special ticket designed for EYT by the association of European Railways.[34]

6

Miscellaneous Developments

TRANSFRONTIER PROPERTY TRANSACTIONS

As has been pointed out elsewhere holidays are no longer the exclusive privilege of a small elite. For better or for worse mass tourism is the feature of today. More than 10 per cent of the entire British population took holidays in Spain in 1987 and 180 million EC citizens now take their holidays away from home.[1] Many of them attracted by the climate, the quality of life and the low cost of living have decided to buy a house or flat in other Member States as a holiday home or retirement home. Spain alone has one million foreign-owned properties along the Mediterranean coast: some 200,000 Britons, a great number of Germans, Scandinavians, Dutch and Danes are permanently living there. In 1986 property buyers provided 12 per cent of total tourist income in Spain. Apparently, in reality, the percentage is even higher since many properties are undervalued to evade tax. Usually the buying of foreign property causes few problems. Sometimes however foreign property buyer's dreams of living in the sun turn into nightmares. As the McMillan Scott report puts it, they lose their villa or flat and their life savings through fraud and inefficiency or because they fail to take legal advice, or at least they suffer an unending bureaucracy. Many victims have addressed themselves to the European Parliament, to Mr Edward McMillan Scott and to the European Commission's DG responsible for consumer protection. The report furthermore points out that the implications of the 1992 programme for transfrontier property transactions are profound and include: mutual recognition of professional qualifications (lawyers, notaries, estate agents, architects, surveyors, etc.), liberalization of exchange controls; proposed EC legislation on unfair contract terms; EC misleading advertising rules; EC Mortgage credit and other financial services legislation (solvency, pensions, insurance, etc.); EC construction products directive and building standards rules; free movement of personal goods; and EC right of residence legislation. Therefore the report aims to examine the sort of problems that can arise, to consider actions currently being taken and to examine ways to create a number of minimum safeguards for prospective purchasers. A transfrontier property transaction is defined as negotiations for the sale or purchase of real property involving the nationals or the legal systems of two or more Member States.

The majority of the complaints relate to properties in Spain (90 per cent). Except for some isolated complaints regarding France, Greece, Italy and Malta, the remainder concern Portugal. With regard to fraud, since the situation is the most serious there, the rapporteur has concentrated on Spain and Portugal. The petitions and complainants are predominantly German, Dutch, British, Belgian or French. It also appears that Northern Europeans are also often responsible for the malpractices. The rapporteur complains about slack attitudes to planning, construction quality, professional standards and fiscal correctness as well as high commission rates and instant profit and describes the sector as dominated by greed.

Examples of practices

Several specific cases of fraud and dishonest practices are set out in detail in the report such as the case of Mr and Mrs Byrne who contracted through an English solicitor to buy an apartment in Tenerife from a German developer. It appeared that there were two owners and the signatures of both were required. Consequently the Byrnes do not have the title deeds. Moreover. the development was built without planning consent. It is therefore illegal and it lacks water and electricity.[2] Such illegal developments apparently are quite common along the Mediterranean and Atlantic coasts. Often speculators buy (cheaper) agricultural land and build on it in the hope that planning consent will follow.

The report illustrates the problem also with the case of Mr and Mrs Lüssman.[3] The house the plaintiff acquired was not only in a completely ruinous state, but built on an illegal housing estate where the same developer had built over seventy buildings without planning permission or the required technical building plans. The distressed Mr and Mrs Lüssman returned to Germany where Mrs Lüssman recently died. As the report points out hidden mortgages, debts and tax liabilities present also problems. It appears that under the present rules it is not the task of the notary in Spain to verify whether the property is free from encumbrances, nor to offer advice to the parties. Many of the sad cases referred to the rapporteur are the result of misunderstanding of the role of the notary or the purchaser's failure to make the necessary checks himself. Other problems concern defective construction as in the case of the Lüssmans or difficulties with the local authorities. The rapporteur believes that many of these problems would be reduced if foreign residents were entitled to vote in local and European elections. Redress through legal action in the Courts of the Countries concerned does not appear to be the solution because of delays and high costs. Often in the end litigants have turned to the European Parliament out of despair of the law's delays. High pressure selling with or without low-cost 'inspection flights' are another problem.

Timeshares

High pressure selling is also causing great problems in relation to time share properties.

Mr McMillan Scott has pressed the European Commission to include a cooling-off period in the Unfair Contract Terms Directive which is making its way through the EC legislative process.[4] If timeshare purchasers had the right to change their minds the intensive selling after people have been attracted to the premises of the timeshare marketing companies with offers of luxury awards would be negated. The proposal for a Directive on unfair terms in consumer contracts contains a provision relating to timeshare contracts to the effect that any such contract which does not provide for the consumer purchaser to 'cool off' within seven days, shall be treated as unfair.[5] The Commission has promised to organize an open conference in Brussels, for analysis of the consumers problem in purchasing immovable property in another Member State (including timeshare purchasing).

In England the Timeshare Developers Association was formed recently after pressure on the industry to put its house in order. Mr McMillan Scott feels that the rules governing timeshare activities constitute progress and could usefully be applied to the transfrontier property sector as a whole. Ten per cent of the complaints received by the rapporteur were concerned with timeshare problems.

Not many problems solved

In very few cases the problem has been resolved. There has been little response from national civil servants. A working group set up by the Spanish government has pointed out that less than 1 per cent of complaints involved organs of the Spanish government and that, therefore, most disputes were a matter of private law. The Spanish government, however, is not ignoring the problem. For example, the Ministries for Tourism, Consumer Protection and Public Works have jointly published a pamphlet in six languages to provide guidance in respect of the acquisition of real estate in Spain. The Generalitat of Catalunya has done the same. The Defensor del pueblo ('Ombudsman') has also been very helpful. The foreign property owners institute (Instituto de proprietarios extranjeros s.a.) also has been of assistance and has drawn attention to the difficulties experienced by foreigners wishing to purchase property in Spain. The rapporteur also endorses the proposals for tackling the problem of fraud put forward by COAPI (Colegio Oficial de Agentes de la Propriedad Immobiliaria de Alicante y su provincia).

Unfortunately, in respect of fraud and malpractice. there are too few examples of successful prosecution both in Mediterranean and Northern European countries.

EC and transfrontier property transactions

The Commission has given some time and effort to the problem. For example, it has held meetings with national officials and has invited their co-operation in improving administrative practice. However it did not go as far as setting up, as it was asked to do, a special task force to deal with fraud, mortgages, defective deeds, faulty construction, etc.

Mr Garcia Amigo in his report on timesharing has proposed an EC Directive.[6] Mr McMillan Scott endorses this approach and favours a Directive safeguarding the rights of property buyers as consumers and an Internal Market for property. He is confident that an adequate legal base exists for EC legislation in this field. Property buyers are to be seen as consumers and are therefore entitled to the protection of EC law. Article 18 of the SEA explicitly brings consumer protection into the scope of the Treaty (100 A EEC). The report mentions the following essential minimum provisions of a future directive on transfrontier property transactions or amendments to existing legislation:

(1) a cooling-off period during which a purchaser may rescind the contract and obtain repayment in full of all monies paid to the vendor or his agent. Such a seven-day cooling-off period is also found in Directive (85/577/EEC) on the protection of the consumer in respect of contracts negotiated away from business premises. This Directive applies to contracts concluded during an excursion organized by the trader away from his business premises, but expressly excludes contracts for the construction, sale and rental of immovable property;[7]

(2) misleading advertising/unfair contract terms. A contract or its terms should be considered unfair and therefore voidable if:
 – it contains stipulations contrary to the law of the land
 – the avoidance of tax is implicit in the terms of the contract;

(3) vendors must hold purchasers money in a joint or trust account;

(4) compulsory insurance by the developer or his agents against the risk of being unable to complete the development for economic reasons;

(5) a standard form contract should be available in the nine official EC languages;

(6) a disclaimer should be included in any advertising for properties not yet built or inviting investors, stating that professional advice is recommended.

The report also makes some general recommendations. Buyers should engage independent professionals to be responsible for ascertaining matters such as: registration of the property, checking who the owner is, whether there are any taxes, duties, mortgages or other charges that may be due, whether the property has been built in accordance with planning regulations, and whether there is a certificate re water, gas and electricity installations, etc.

The rapporteur furthermore suggests that the inclusion of a certified copy of the entry in the land register in the documents to be produced before the notary prior to the preparation of the 'escritura' (title deeds) could avoid many problems.

The EC could also help to fight fraud and malpractice by launching an EC wide publicity campaign as part of its action programme on Consumer Protection and Tourism. Another suggestion is that 'option contracts' which are commonly issued to reserve a property should state that the final contract is 'subject to clear title and free of encumbrances'. The rapporteur would also like to see a European register of persons banned by court order from acting as director of a company registered in one of the Member States.

Other general recommendations concern matters such as:

- closer co-operation between police and criminal justice authorities in the Member States;
- the appointment of a planning officer for illegal developments (to regularize latent illegality of certain properties);
- defective construction (the Defensor del pueblo has proposed that the developer should be held personally and strictly liable for building defects. Prudent developers would then take out an insurance policy to cover themselves against claims by purchasers.);
- legal aid;
- voting rights in local elections.[8]

CONVENTION ON TOURISM

Some attention should also be paid to the International Convention to facilitate travel and tourist stays, which is being drafted within the WTO (World Tourism Organisation).

The EC has participated in the preparatory work on this Convention, particularly in respect of certain matters such as passports, visas, health checks, customs and foreign exchange.[9] It is felt that since some of the matters of the draft Convention fall within the EC's responsibility and since in some areas, such as custom matters, it has sole power the EC as such should be party to the Convention. The European Court, as seen above, has ruled on the status of a tourist and has pointed out that EC nationals going abroad for the purpose of tourism are to be regarded as 'recipients of services'.[10]

Luisi and Carbone were fined for exporting currency from Italy. The Court held, in answer to a request for a preliminary ruling, that Articles 59 and 60 EEC, which govern the freedom to provide services, also cover the receipt of services. So tourists come within the economic scope of the Treaty. Council Directive 73/148 of 21 May 1973[11] laid down at EC level the rules on movement and residence within the EC not only for providers of services but also (and quite explicitly so) for recipients of these.

This directive also covers Members of the families of recipients of services, even if they are not nationals of a Member State. It is, therefore, felt that in areas where the EC exercises its powers the Member States may no longer adopt provisions in an International Convention which are inconsistent with their Treaty obligations. The Commission has requested the Council to authorize it to take part, on behalf of the EC, in the negotiations concerning the drafting of this WTO Convention, which will be open for accession by the EC and its Member States. The Secretary General of the WTO has no objections to the opening of the Convention for signature by regional economic integration organizations such as the EC and has, therefore, asked the secretariat to pursue its contacts with the Commission in this respect.

The Convention is to facilitate travel and tourist stays. The Commission has proposed to the Council to decide that the Member States shall adopt a joint position on matters that do not fall within the competence of the EC.

HOTEL KEEPING CONTRACTS

Not only the EC but other bodies, such as the Council of Europe and Unidroit, have been active in the sphere of tourism, travel and the hotel industry. However, there has been little enthusiasm for harmonization of hotel keeping contracts.

Unidroit (the International Institute for the Unification of Private Law), for example, was initially responsible for the 1970 International Convention on the Travel Contract.[12] Although this Convention is in force it has met with little success (only two EC Member States, i.e. Belgium and Italy, have ratified it) and it is unlikely to assume an important role in the future development of tourism law in Europe, particularly in view of the EC's Directive on package tours, which was discussed in Chapter 4 and which occupies a central place in the EC's developing policy on tourism.

With regard to hotel keeping contracts, Unidroit has been advocating and endeavouring to secure the adoption worldwide of an International Convention. There is already the 1962 Convention of the Council of Europe which entered into force in February 1967 and has been ratified by the United Kingdom. It was based on a pre-war preliminary draft by Unidroit and deals merely with the hotelkeeper's liability for damage to or loss of property brought to the hotel by guests.[13] Unidroit's more recent activities concern the adoption of a much wider and more comprehensive convention on hotelkeepers' contracts. However, this initiative has met throughout with hostility from the hotelkeeping profession which has insisted that there was no need for a new international instrument in this sphere. Given its poor chances of success and the unjustified imbalance in favour of the guest by which the draft convention was characterized, it was recommended (by the relevant subcommittee of Unidroit) that the draft should be revised in the light of the above-mentioned 1962 Council of Europe Convention and of the International Hotel Regulations of the IHA (the International Hotel Association). It should also be pointed out that governmental support for a new convention has not been enthusiastic.

Meanwhile at its seventieth session, held in May 1991, the Governing Council of Unidroit decided that the present attitude of governments was such that it would be, at the present time, inappropriate to contemplate pursuing work on the draft Convention on the hotelkeepers' contract.

1992 AND THE HOTEL AND CATERING INDUSTRY

Hotrec (the Confederation of National Hotel and Restaurant Associations in the EC) has produced a White Paper, entitled 'The 1992 challenge for the Hotel, Restaurant and Café Industry'. The EC Commission has backed this initiative with financial support. Hotrec, which was also assisted by experts of the Hotel School of the Hague, is a supranational body of twenty-two organizations representing more than a million undertakings. The paper deals with opportunities as well as threats. Strategic implications for both the public and private sector are also dealt with. One of the main findings is that a Community-wide identity of the 'Tourism and hospitality product' has to be created and marketed. The Commission is called upon to encourage the co-ordination of promotional efforts of EC Member States by making a substantial budget available. Hotrec could play a co-ordinating role in respect of a joint promotional campaign for a European Tourism Product.

The Commission is already engaged in providing such assistance, for example with regard to rural tourism.

Hotrec has also pleaded for a reduced VAT tariff in respect of goods and services of the tourism and hospitality industry. It is felt that placing such products and services in the standard tariff would be detrimental for the sector's competitive position and would have serious negative effects on employment. In most Member States hotel, restaurant and café goods and services are taxed according to a reduced VAT rate. It is, furthermore, pointed out that the unification process may encourage investment in the hospitality industry as well as more co-operation, mergers, takeovers and monopolistic reservation systems. Small businesses will not be as well placed to attract venture capital as the bigger ones and the competitive position of smaller businesses will deteriorate as a result of these developments. Therefore smaller hotels and restaurants are encouraged not only to utilize the better opportunities for investment, in particular by upgrading the quality of their product, but also to co-operate with regard to promotion, reservation systems, information systems and perhaps even the purchasing of goods. Hotrec could co-ordinate an open European reservation system for hotels. Another important matter dealt with is standardization. At present there is no standard definition of tourism, a hotel a restaurant or a café. The EC Commission has been asked to encourage standardization of systems of data collection and criteria. Where data collection is done by governments, the EC could issue Directives; where it is the task of the organizations in the industry the EC could give advice.[14] Hotrec should prepare an annual monograph on European tourism and the hotel and catering industry.

Part two of the present White Paper (dealing with the hotel and restaurant industry) in fact can be seen as the first such monograph. The information given to consumers also needs to be standardized. Hotrec has developed a standard Information System for the hospitality industry to be used in all Member States on its own or in combination with existing systems. This standard information system has been approved by the EC Council of Ministers.[15]

As has been done by the Commission and the Economic and Social Committee, Hotrec stresses the importance of EC initiatives to improve transport infrastructure and to safeguard the environment. Not only physical pollution (air, water and ground) is envisaged but also 'cultural pollution' (loss of identity due to mass tourism). Both forms can destroy tourism since they remove the incentive to travel.

The White Paper also deals with the problem of manpower demand. The hospitality industry may have to compete for labour, since the employment pool of young workers (on which it heavily depends) is about to shrink in the near future. It is hoped that use can be made of the expected increase in interstate mobility of labour. Finally it is felt that education and training institutes in the hotel and catering industry should be stimulated by Hotrec to develop an accreditation system, opening doors to the recognition of diplomas among the Member States. The Commission is asked to encourage the industry to train their staff in languages. Very useful in this respect could be the European hotel trainee placement scheme.[16] The ESC has welcomed this scheme but it feels that it needs further development and extension to other sectors of the tourist industry. This interesting paper not only contains a great deal of information concerning the unification process, but it also calls for action and provides suggestions for strategic directions to be further developed and executed by private as well as public organizations at national and EC level.

7
Conclusion

Tourism and the EC's activities in respect of it have come a long way. Travel and tourism is now the world's biggest single industry employing more than 112 million people and producing nearly £100 billion per year in taxes.[1] It accounts for between 25 and 30 per cent of world trade in services.[2]

In the EC also the importance of tourism is growing and the EC, as has been described above, has indeed not been idle in this field. Of course it has also had its setbacks as a result of events such as the Chernobil accident, the Libyan raid and more recently the Gulf War and the recession. In the EC tourism in all its components is now the largest single industry in the European economy. Once the negative consequences of the Gulf War will have been overcome tourism will be able to flourish and develop fully again but it should not be overlooked that tourism in Europe has lost 10 per cent of its world market share in the last decade and that it continues to decline in relative terms.[3]

However, as pointed out above, the EC is in the process of developing a common policy. As long as the Community in one way or another makes available the necessary funds and, as on the whole it seems to be doing, develops the right policies and drafts proper legislation to deal with inadequacies, it is not so serious that tourism has not yet been formally incorporated as such into the EC's powers and responsibility under the Treaties.[4] It is slightly odd, to say the least, that so far the EC's largest single economic activity is not formally recognized as an area of competence. The Commission has resorted to the subsidiarity principle to explain its failure to act in this respect.[5]

If policies such as the one on the environment can be Treaty based there is no reason why tourism policy objectives should not be pursued at European level. However, meanwhile in 1989 the Commission has set up a new Directorate General DG XXIII to deal with tourism *inter alia*, which, since February 1990, is being directed by the experienced, highly competent and effective German Lawyer Heinrich von Moltke (who used to be deputy head of the EC Mission in Washington and for six years Chef de cabinet of Commissioner Narjes, and prior to his appointment, deputy Director General for industrial affairs and the Internal Market). The latest action programme, discussed in Chapter 5, is an early example of the efforts of the new Directorate General. It is a good start which gently and gradually paves the way for a Community tourism policy. Among those calling for a Treaty-based policy on tourism are the European Chambers of Commmerce.[6] Eurochambers, the European Association of Chambers of Commerce and Industry have called on the EC and national bodies to set up a real European policy on tourism, aimed in particular, at the suppression of the distortion of competition as a result of national legislation in the services area and the social and taxation burdens that hinder Community exchanges.

FUTURE OF TOURISM

Until recently EC policy has been heavily concentrated on consumer protection. The Economic and Social Committee as well as the European Parliament have stressed the need for a serious examination of the future of tourism and its contribution to regional development in its widest sense, including town and country planning, where relevant.[7] This EC advisory organ has also justly stressed the need for a more comprehensive policy which would underline the economic and social importance of tourism in the sphere of regional policy and job creation.

In Chapter 5 it was also pointed out how tourism has not only increasingly become dependent on several other EC policies such as transport, the environment, social development, agriculture, services etc., but also how other policies are affected by it. Therefore it is imperative that, as increasingly happens and has been demonstrated above, EC policies must take tourist developments fully into consideration. The link between tourism and the environment, in particular, is being stressed increasingly. Local and regional authorities as well as businesses are involved with Tourism. The hotel and catering industry is, of course, the obvious example but other businesses such as commerce, the crafts industry and agriculture are indirectly involved. The Economic and Social Committee in particular has underlined that not only agricultural but also industrial areas wishing to diversify are relevant to tourism and that the best approach to tourism policy is to make use of the subsidiarity principle.

CRISIS

Tourism is not only in a state of development but is also in a crisis situation. As was seen in Chapters 1, 2 and 5 a new approach is being advocated and developed to overcome problems such as overcrowding, over-exploitation and environmental damage as well as cultural impoverishment. The Economic and Social Committee has advocated the development of quality in tourism by measures such as investment in infrastructure in resorts hit by the crisis in growth, regulations to preserve and raise standards, refurbishment of old hotel accommodation and restoration of old buildings.[8] This is undoubtedly the right approach. Support must also be given to the measures discussed above in relation to the staggering of holidays and the development of alternative forms of tourism.

ACHIEVEMENTS

As was pointed out, particularly in Chapters 3 and 4, a great deal has already been done to put tourism policy on the map such as the adoption of general Internal Market measures in the sphere of transport, tax, company law, the right of establishment and the freedom to provide services, the free movement of capital, competition policy and social policy. Or action undertaken in the context of policies in the sphere of enterprise policy, regional policy, consumer protection, agriculture, culture, the environment and education. Or finally through direct measures such as those described in Chapters 3 and 4 (and the important package travel Directive in particular).

SHORTCOMINGS

However, in order to achieve a truly Single Market in Tourism much more remains to be done.[9]

The ESC mentions in particular:

- common regulations to protect tourists from profiteers, other sources of harassment and incorrect information;
- standardization of the categorization of tourist accommodation (number of stars etc., see Chapter 4);
- minimum requirements for standard contracts (governing relations between hoteliers, transporters and tour operators, tour operators and sales agencies, and relations with customers at all stages);
- the interoperability of credit cards and electronic means of payment and the promotion of the ECU;
- an effective pan-European air traffic control system;
- a common policy to protect tourists from terrorism.

Other shortcomings pointed at by the ESC include:[10]

- staff shortages in DG XXIII with consequent loss of co-ordination with other DGs;
- lack of co-ordination among the structural funds aimed at strengthening the tourism sector and solving its problems;
- lack of protection from unfair competition caused by differences in exchange rates and other technical barriers;
- too little encouragement to gain closer knowledge of the culture and the way of life of the Member States;
- insufficient consideration given to some new forms of tourism such as cultural and social tourism;
- not sufficient protection of intra-Community tourism;
- insufficient protection against overbooking.

Some progress in certain areas has been made particularly in respect of the latter criticism but, unfortunately, one has to admit that most of the other criticisms relating to lack of progress are not totally unfounded as has been illustrated throughout this work.

The European Parliament feels, *inter alia*, that in the creation of a single market positive action is required to assist firms and SMEs in particular.[11] It has also called on the Intergovernmental Conference on political union to consider the explicit incorporation of tourism into the Treaties as an essential flanking policy for the creation of Economic and Monetary Union even if the treaty rules on the freedoms in the Internal Market also embrace tourism. It is, furthermore, important as the European Parliament has pointed out that DG XXIII strengthens its horizontal role to ensure that tourism interests are properly represented in policies promoted by other DGs.[12] The Parliament has also asked the Commission to help develop European training schemes for tourism industry professions. There is also scope for improvement in the transport sector.[13] The Parliament has welcomed Council Regulation No. 2299/89 of 24 July 1989 on a code of conduct for computerized reservation systems[14] since this will prevent distortion of competition and it has urged the Commission to take steps to create uniform conditions to govern the licensing of travel agencies and a code of conduct for travel agents based on the principles of neutral, comprehensive, accurate and transparent information offered to the consumer, but also urged to give some thought to how this Directive is to be co-ordinated with national law.[15]

Although the Parliament welcomes Council Regulation (EEC) No 295/91 of 4 February 1991[16] establishing common rules for a denied boarding compensation system in scheduled air transport, it calls on the Commission to ensure that airlines meet the provisions concerning compensation procedures for passengers who have been denied authorisation to board an overbooked flight.

In respect of youth tourism, the Parliament has reiterated its request for the introduction of a European young person's travel card.[17] It has also called on the Commission to promote sport-related tourism. It has further requested the Commission to make specific proposals to apply the principles of the proposed Directive (discussed in Chapter 3 p. 57) on atypical work to cover seasonal workers in the tourist industry having regard to their particular needs and circumstances and urges the Member States and the Commission to begin work on better vocational training of seasonal staff.[18] The Parliament, not unreasonably, also calls for a systematic information policy and has pointed at several shortcomings remaining in the sphere of consumer protection. For example, it has invited the Commission to submit a proposal for a regulation on the protection of establishments offering accommodation, campsites and discothèques against fire risks further to the recommendation of 22 December 1986.[19] The Parliament also feels that a harmonized system of grading for hotels, boarding houses, hostels and other establishments offering accommodation based on objective criteria must be established. It furthermore, rightly, calls for the replacement of the system of form E111 by more efficient and comprehensive measures including a more comprehensive system for holiday insurance when booked on a package holiday. Other important and interesting improvements called for by the European Parliament include a compensation scheme for tourists who are not only victims of crime but have also suffered bodily harm as a result of a criminal act.

As was pointed out in Chapter 6, the Parliament also calls for much needed progress with the drafting of EC rules on cross-border real estate transactions and for a comprehensive Directive on timeshares. The Commission should also start work on the possibilities of redress for tourists and it is, furthermore, important that the Commission undertakes an examination of the role and functions of credit card payment systems as they apply in the tourism sector. The Parliament has also drafted a charter on the rights and obligations of tourists[20] and has asked the Commission to use this as the basis for a proposal to the Council for a Directive on this subject. Lastly, the Parliament is right to remind the Commission of the crucial importance of the liberalization of passenger transport for tourism.[21]

FINANCING

The EC's structural funds (as seen above in Chapter 2) provide considerable finance for projects of importance for tourism, both directly (marinas, conference centres, etc.) and indirectly (roads, electricity, water supply). Since the reform of the structural funds in 1989 the contributions have been doubled from 1987 to 1993[22] from some 7 billion ECU to 14 billion ECU.

In the Community Support Frameworks negotiated within the partnership for the less favoured regions of the EC more than 2 billion ECU will be allocated directly to tourism developments over the period 1989–93, most of which from the ERDF. This amount represents about 6 per cent of EC assistance in these regions over the period 1989–93. The structural funds furthermore contribute substantially in these regions to the development of basic infrastructure such as transport, energy and water supplies. In the Integrated Mediterranean Programmes tourism accounts for 13 per cent of total expenditure. ENVIREG, in contributing to the reduction of pollution in coastal zones, will have a beneficial impact on the tourist industry and many other EC programmes can contribute to tourism activities.

The development of rural tourism will also create new economic activities and boost local employment. The European Investment Bank can also be of assistance in respect of loans for hotels and tourist facilities, which could be of particular interest to SMEs, which are such a common feature in the tourist trade. The ESC has called for a doubling of the structural funds to be used to influence investments in tourist facilities and it has pointed out that only a small proportion of EC funds is specifically allocated to tourism.[23] It is not, however, generally in favour of support for isolated projects or piecemeal development and it feels that there should only be assistance from the structural funds where there is evidence of a framework plan (discussed by responsible authorities, developers, entrepreneurs and social partners) to which participants are prepared to make a substantial commitment.

It would be wrong to state, despite the small percentage allocated directly to tourism and the Member States instinctive reticence in respect of subsidies, that the total direct and indirect EC funding taken together with national direct and indirect aid is insignificant. More recently on 13 July 1992 the Council adopted a Decision on a Community action plan to assist tourism (see OJ. No L 231/26 of 13 August 1992). The EC financial resources deemed necessary for its implementation amount to 18 million ECU and shall fall within the Community financial framework in force. Measures, which must be consistent with the sibsidiarity principle, must be cost effective and make a significant impact on the EC tourist industry. They must facilitate the development of the industry with particular reference to SMEs. They must help improve the quality of EC tourist services and encourage competition within the EC as well as increase competitiveness of EC tourist services on the world market. Measures must furthermore be conducive to the preservation and protection of the quality of the natural environment, the cultural heritage and the integrity of local populations. They must also contribute to improving the provision of information and services and to the protection of tourists.

PARLIAMENT'S ROLE

Finally, it should be stressed that one of the most staunch supporters of an EC policy on tourism is the European Parliament. Mr Edward McMillan Scott, MEP, in particular deserves praise.[24] Although Mr McMillan Scott continues to express his strong support for the development of an EC tourism policy in co-operation with the Member States he has been quite severe in his criticism of the management of the EYT by both the Commission and the national tourist authorities. He feels that repeated warnings by Parliament about possible failure were ignored.[25]

Mr McMillan Scott is the co-ordinator of the 'Umbrella Europe' campaign for travellers' rights in Europe, which focuses attention on issues such as health care, air fares, package holidays, insurance, travel allowances, guarantees in respect of goods bought abroad, homes abroad, safety (coaches, cars, hotels, drinking water, bathing water, mugging, theft, terrorism), frontier controls and traveller rights and privileges.

An interesting recent EP initiative is concerned with the establishment of a European register of travel agencies.[26] The motion calls for such register to contain precise and specific details of the character, legal personality, the extent of its operations and its commercial liability and recommends that any travel agency which has committed commercially improper acts be noted as such in the European register of travel agencies as a way of warning the European tourist industry not to trade with such an offending agency.

Another recent initiative calls on the Commission to draw up a Directive harmonizing and simplifying camping car tourism on the basis of the particular characteristics of camping cars and the specific needs involved.[27]

The machine is grinding on. No one would have believed in 1958 that one day there would be sufficient material to dedicate an entire book to the EC's activities and law relating to tourism. The moment for a proper EC policy has, however, arrived and in a way, since tourism is so pervasive in respect of other policies activities and rules, the process is unstoppable. The incubation period, as seen above, has been remarkably short. Most has been achieved over the last ten years or so. As pointed out previously all EC institutions, including the Court of Justice, have played their role.

Whether there will be a formal tourism policy might merely be a matter of time and from the substantive point of view the question is not a crucial one, since tourism is deeply interwoven with so many other policies. Tourism can even act as a catalyst in other areas where progress is blocked. However, Community support and finance are as vital, if not more so, as the question of formal incorporation. One must hope that the latest action plan will eventually bring all it promises to fruition. Certainly the degree of success already achieved with the completion of the Internal Market is of great benefit to tourism.

Notes

1: Introduction

1 See, e.g., the Commission's initial guidelines for a Community policy on tourism, *EC Bull* supp. 4/82.
2 See EP Resolution, OJ 1984 C 10. Motion for a Resolution by the EP's Committee on Youth; report by E. Brook on a People's Europe, PE 99624, 8 October 1985.
3 See COM(86) 32 final, p. 4.
4 See Council Resolution on a Community policy on tourism, OJ 1984 C115.
5 See European File 1990, 2/90 p. 3 and CES 1063/90 p. 9.
6 Ibid. p. 3.
7 See COM(91) 97 final, p. 3.
8 Ibid. p. 2.
9 See *European File* No 9/87.
10 See Frans van Kraay, *Law for Business* July 1991, p. 344 *et seq*. and 'Tourism and regional development', ESC 1990, p. 9.
11 See Chapter 3.
12 See note 10.
13 See *EC Bull* supp. 4/82.
14 See ESC 'Opinion on tourism', 1984, p. 1.
15 See Chapter 5, p. 100 for more details.
16 See 'Community action in the field of tourism', COM(86) 32 final, p. 1.)
17 'ESC opinion onCommunity action in the field of Tourism' OJ 1986 C 328/ p. 2.
18 See note 14.
19 See COM(91) 97 final, pp. 4, 5.

2: Initial objectives and themes of action

1 See COM(86) 32 final and European File 9/87 May 1987.
2 See Resolution on facilitation, promotion and funding of tourism in the European Community, OJ 1988 C 49/157.

3 See *EC Bull* supp. 2/88, ‘A People’s Europe’, p. 17.
4 Ibid. p. 17 and OJ 1984 C 159, *EC Bull* 6 – 1984, point 15. 1 *et seq.*
5 OJ 1985 C 47; OJ 1985 C 131.
6 See Completing the Internal Market, the Elimination of frontier Controls.
7 See *EC Bull* supp. 2/88.
8 See ISEC/B5/90 p. 5, European File 9/87 p. 5 and OJ 1985 C 47.
9 See Target 92, No 1 1991 p. 3.
10 See ISEC/B9/90.
11 See Target 92, No 5 1991 p. 2.
12 For further details on tax free allowances see: Council Directives 85/348; 87/198; 88/664: OJ 1985 L 183; OJ 1987 L 77; OJ 1988 382. For further details on tax paid allowances see Commission proposal COM(89) 331/11 final; OJ 1989 C 245 and amended proposal COM(90) 76 final OJ 1990 C 70.
13 See note 7.
14 See Target 92 No 2, 1991.
15 See SME Euro-Info 31/90/EN p. 1.
16 See Target 92, No 1 1991.
17 See *Single Market News* Autumn 1991, p. 10 and supp.
18 See Frans van Kraay, *Law for Business*, 1992, p. 78 *et seq.*
19 See Council Directive 72/166 on the approximation of the laws of the Member States relating to insurance against civil liability in respect of the use of motor vehicles and to the enforcement of the obligation to insure against such liability; OJ 1972 L 103.
20 See Commission Recommendation 81/76, OJ 1981 L 57.
21 Council Directive 84/5, OJ 1984 L 8.
22 See Frans van Kraay, *Law for Business*, April 1991, p. 219 *et seq.*
23 Directive 90/232, OJ 1990 L 129.
24 On common position see note 22 and for Directive 88/357 see OJ 1988 L 172.
25 See Frans van Kraay, *Law for Business*, August/September 1991, p. 384.
26 First Council Directive 80/1263, OJ 1980 L 375 p. 1.
27 See OJ No C 48/1 and COM(90) 513 final and EP briefing PE 142, 195 p. 1.
28 See note 17, supp.
29 On the Uniform Passport see Resolution of the representatives of the governments of the Member States, meeting within the Council, OJ 1981 C 241/ 1 and the resolution on the adoption of a passport of uniform pattern, OJ 1982, C 179/1.
30 Resolution on facilitation, promotion and funding of tourism DOC AZ -209/87 OJ C 49/160.
31 For more details see Chapter 3.

32 See *EC Bull* supp. 4/86 p. 7.
33 OJ 1989 C 69, p. 213 and PE 146.115/final, p. 17.
34 See ESC opinion on Community Action in the filed of tourism OJ 1986 C 328/3.
35 See ESC opinion on tourism, Brussels, February 1984, p. 21, and ISEC/B5/90, p. 5.
36 See European File 9/87, p. 7; OJ 1984 No C, p. 7 and ESC opinion on draft Council recommendation on the adoption of a European emergency health card; OJ 1984 No C 206/11.
37 See also Council resolution on a European emergency health card, OJ 1986 C 184/4 and written question No 487/89 OJ 1990 C 69/14 and CES 257/90 final, p. 27.
38 See OJ 1986 C 184/5–15.
39 See COM(86) 32 final, p. 7.
40 See Chapter 4.
41 See note 34, OJ 1986 C 328/3.
42 See Council Directive 88/361 for the implementation of Article 67 EEC, OJ 1988 L 178.
43 See COM(89) 60 final, OJ 1989 C 141.
44 OJ 1986 L 332.
45 OJ 1985 L 372.
46 For more details see 'Completing the Internal Market, capital movements', Vol. 1 December 1990, p. 105 *et seq*.
47 See COM(90) 106 final, OJ 1990 C 106 and Frans van Kraay, *Law for Business* March 1991, p. 178.
48 See note 17.
49 For more details see Frans van Kraay, *Law for Business*, April 1991, p. 159.
50 Commission Recommendation 90/109: OJ 1990 L 67/39, discussed in *Law for Business*, January 1991, p. 90.
51 See PE 146, 115 final, p. 22.
52 Cases 286/82 and 26/83 Luisi and Carbone v Ministero del Tesoro [1984] ECR 377, [1985] 3 CMLR 52.
53 See background report ISEC/B33/91, p. 9.
54 See COM(91) 97 final p. 4.
55 See background Report ISEC/B33/91, p. 9.
56 See note 52 and see also dicta in 118/75 re Watson and Belmann (1976) ECR 1185; (1976) 2 CMLR 552.
57 See Cowan v Le Trésor Public, case 186/87 [1990] CMLR 613.
58 See Directive 64/220 (and Directive 73/148) concerning the abolition of restrictions on movement and residence within the EC for nationals of Member States with regard to the establishment and the provision of services: Dir. 64/220, OJ 1963–1964, 115 (JO 845/1964); Dir. 73/148; OJ 1973 L 172/14.

59 See M. Bogdan, 'Free movement of tourists within the EEC', *JWTL* (1977) 468 *et seq.*
60 See van der Woude and Mead, 'Free movement of tourists', *CML Rev* (1988), 123 *et seq.*
61 See ISEC/B21/91, 24 July 1991, p. 3.
62 See European File 9/87, May 1987, p. 7.
63 COM(86) 32 final.
64 Council Directive 85/337, OJ 1988 L 175.
65 See Annex COM(86) 32 final and CES 257/90 final appendix 2, p. 59.
66 OJ 1984 C 115.
67 For further details see results of the international conference 'Improving seasonal spread of tourism', 16 and 17 October 1991 Noordwijk, Netherlands.
68 See answer to parliamentary question No 2365/90 OJ 1991 C 323/1.
69 See OJ 1986 C 328, p. 1 *et seq.*
70 For more details see COM(86) 52 final.
71 See note 32, p. 10.
72 See OJ 1985 L 197.
73 See note 32, p. 10.
74 See written question No 1088/90 OJ 1990 C 283/34.
75 See background report ISEC/B28/90, 26 October 1990 and COM(90) 438.
76 See note 32, p. 10.
77 See OJ 1985 L 93; OJ 1980 L 180; OJ 1988 L 102; OJ 1986 L 128.
78 See SEC(90) 1602 final.
79 See note 32, p. 10.
80 See *EIB Information* October 1986, No 50, p. 10.
81 See 'Tourism and Regional Development', *ESC* 1990, p. 10.
82 Ibid. p. 11.
83 See COM(86) 32 final, EC action in the field of tourism p. 13.
84 See note 34.
85 See *EIB Information* October 1986 No 50, p. 9 *et seq.*
86 For details on financing for infrastructure, see *EIB Information* No 49, 1 July 1986 and for more details on the ways in which the *EIB* supports the development of tourism see *EIB Information* December 1989 no 62 p. 4 *et seq.*
87 See note 85 and for details of the gobal loan facility, see *EIB Information* Nos 24, 30, 35 and 36.
88 For more detaiks see note 85.
89 See DOC A2–209/87, OJ 1988 C 49/162.
90 See ESC Opinion, OJ 1986 C 328/1 and note 81, p. 35
91 See note 81, p. 13.
92 See note 54, p. 33
93 See note 91, p. 35.

94 See note 51, p. 8.
95 See note 62, p. 9.
96 See OJ 1986 L 384/54, and OJ 1986 C 114/8; see also Chapter 4.
97 See note 63, p. 15.
98 See European File 9/87 May 1987
99 See note 32, p. 12.
100 See OJ 1986 L 384/60, and OJ 1984 C 49.
101 See note 32, p. 12.
102 See Council Directive 90/314 on package travel, package holidays and package tours, OJ 1990 L 158/59, and for a comment on the proposal for this Directive see Frans van Kraay, *Law for Business*, July 1990, p. 373.
103 See note 51, p. 20
104 See note 32, p. 13.
105 See note 98.
106 See *EC Bull* supp. 4/82 p. 19.
107 See note 32, p. 13.
108 For more details see note 54, p. 7 and OJ 1989 C 166/1. On vocational training see also Chapter 5, p. 93 and Chapter 3, p. 62.
109 See note 32, p. 13.
110 See notc 54, p. 7.
111 See C 154/89 Commission v France, C 180/89 Commission v Italy, C 198/89 Commission v Greece. Proceedings of the ECJ 25 February–1 March 1991.
112 See case 168/85 Commission v. Italian Republic, [1986], ECR 2945.
113 See joined cases C 100 and 101/89 Peter Kaefer and Andrea Procacci v French Republic, [1990], ECR I 4647.
114 See note 54, p. 7.
115 OJ 1968 L 260.
116 OJ 1975 L 167.
117 See OJ 1982 L 213/1, Council Directive on measures to facilitate the effective exercise of freedom of establishment and freedom to provide services in respect of activities of self-employed persons in certain services incidental to transport and travel agencies (ISIC group 718) and in storage and warehousing (ISIC group 720) 82/470/EEC.
118 OJ 1981 L 143.
119 See Council Directive 89/48 OJ 1989 L19/16 and for a comment see Frans van Kraay, 'A single market for the professions', *Law for Business*, November 1990, p. 45.
120 See COM(89) 372 final SYN 209 and CES 86/90, *Bulletin of the ESC* No 2/90. During the Dutch Presidency progress was made in respect of this second diplomas Directive, See *Single Market News*, No 14, Spring 1992, p. 2.

121 OJ 1975 L 167/33.
122 See note 54, p. 7.
123 For more details see D. Lasok, *The Professions and Services in the European Economic Community* (Kluwer (1986), p. 148.
124 OJ 1968, L 260/19; OJ 1968 (II).
125 See Commission Recommendation 69/175, OJ 1969, L 146/7
126 For more details see the annex to this Directive (OJ 1975, L167/33) and D. Lasok, op cit, p. 150.
127 See OJ 1968 L 257, p. 2.
128 See Case C-306/89; Commission v Hellenic Republic, OJ 1992 C 10/8 and Proceedings ECJ 2–13 December 1991, no 22/91.
129 See note 106, p. 20 and 21.
130 Council Regulation No 1302/78 on the granting of financial support for demonstration projects to exploit alternative energy sources; OJ 1978 L 158.
131 Ibid.
132 See note 32, p. 13.
133 See OJ 1986 L 384/52.
134 See OJ 1986 C340/1.
135 See OJ 1990 C 150/4, and written question No 2600/90, OJ 1991 C 107/27.
136 See Chapter 1 and note 98, p. 10.
137 See note 32, p. 14.
138 OJ 1984 C 115.
139 OJ 1986 L 384/52.
140 See written question 2600/90, OJ 1991 C 107/27.

3: Action already taken

1 See COM(91) 97 final, 24 April 1991, p. 6.
2 See Initial Guidelines, Community policy on tourism OJ No C 115/2 *et seq*. 30 April 1984.
3 See European File 9/90, p. 4 *et seq.*
4 See Case No 13/83 European Parliament v. EC Council [1985] ECR 1513 [1986] ICMLR, 138; for a comment see Frans van Kraay JALT 1986, p. 206 *et seq.*
5 For a summary of the state of play with regard to the various areas of transport policy: sea, waterways, road, railways and air see European File 9/90; for more details see Rosa Greaves, *Transport Law of the European Community* (1991).
6 Council Regulation 117/66, OJ 1966 L 147.
7 Council Regulation 517/72, OJ 1972 L 67.
8 See Council Regulation 3022/77 amending Regulation 517/72 OJ 1977 L 358.
9 Council Regulation 516/72, OJ 1972 L 671.

10 See ASOR: Accord Services Occasionels par Route, OJ 1982 L 230.
11 See OJ 1987 C 120, and for amended and re-examined proposal OJ 1988 C 301, and OJ 1989 C 31; see also EP opinion of 10 March 1988 – Wijsenbeek and PE 146/115//rev/Bp. 29.
12 See OJ 1987 C 77, and OJ 1988 C 301.
13 See OJ 1974 L 308/18 and OJ 1974 L 308/23.
14 See Directive 77/796; OJ 1977 L 334/37 and Directive 89/438; OJ 1989 L 212/101.
15 See Directive 85/3; OJ 1985, L2/14 amended by Directive 86/360, OJ 86 L217/19, 86/364, OJ 1986 L 221/48; Dir. 88/218, OJ 1988 L98/48; Dir. 89/338, OJ 1989 L 142/3; Dir 89/461 OJ 1989 L 226/7.
16 Regulation 1463/70 OJ 1970, L 164/1; amended by Reg. 1787/73, OJ 1973 L 181/1; amended by Reg. 2828/77, OJ 1977, L 334/5.
17 For further details concerning these developments see note 3, page 7. During the Dutch Presidency a first step was made towards the opening up of the EC's bus and coach markets with a commitment to further liberalization at a later stage. See DTI *Single Market News* No 14 Spring 1992.
18 See note 3, p. 8.
19 See *Bull ESC* 7–8/1990 p. 36 *et seq*. and *ESC* press release PR 31/90, 6 July 1990.
20 See COM(89) 564 final.
21 See note 1, p. 6.
22 See Council Decision 87/602 (on sharing of passenger capacity and market access, OJ 1987 L 374) and Council Directive 87/601 (on fares) OJ 1987 L 374; see also Council Regulation 2343/90 (on sharing of passenger capacity and market access, second phase) OJ 1990 L 217, and Council Regulation 2342/90 (on fares, second phase) OJ 1990 L 217.
23 See Commission Regulation 2672/88, OJ 1988, L 239/13 (re the application of Article 85, 3 to certain categories of agreements relating to computer reservation systems for air transport services), and Regulation 2299/89, OJ 1989, L 220/1 (on a code of conduct for computerized reservation systems).
24 See OJ 1991 L36, p. 5.
25 See note 2, p. 19.
26 See note 3, p. 8.
27 See Ahmed Saeed v. Zentrale Zur Bekämpfung Unlauteren Wettbewerbs case 66/86 [1989] ECR 803, [1990] 4 *CMLR* 102 and for further details and a comment see Frans van Kraay, *Law for Business* September 1989, p. 446.
28 See OJ 1987 L 374.
29 See Ministère Public v. Asjes, Joined cases 209 to 213/84 [1986] ECR 1425, 1457 and see also Reg. 3975 and 3976/87 on the application of

the rules on competition to undertakings in the air transport sector; OJ 1987 L 374; and Commission Regulations 2671 and 2672 and 2673/88 on the application of Article 85(3) to certain agreements and concerted practices in the sphere of air transport, OJ 1988, L 239 p. 9, 13 and 17.

30 See note 3, p. 9.
31 OJ 1990 L 217/8.
32 For a text of this proposal see OJ 1991 C 258/2.
33 See proposal for a Council Regulation on access for carriers to intra-Community air routes, OJ 1991 C 258/10.
34 OJ 1987 L 374, p. 19.
35 OJ 1990 L 217/8.
36 See proposal for a Council Regulation on fares and rates for air services, OJ 1991 C 258/15 *et seq.*
37 See note 34, p. 12.
38 See note 35, p. 1.
39 See note 3, p. 9.
40 See note 1, p. 6; see also Chapter 2 for progress in this direction.
41 See written question No 2344/90; OJ 1991 C 195/4.
42 See European File 17/82 No V/1982, p. 14.
43 PE 146. 115/final, p. 23.
44 See, e.g., the ESC's comments on the application of VAT and excise duties to transport operations under the tax harmonization proposals, OJ 1990 C 112/90, and OJ 1990 C 56/70.
45 See motion for a resolution by Mr Mottola MEP DOC B3 1901/90; PE 146.115/final/annex.
46 See OJ 1990 C 309/6.
47 See *Single Market News* and Supplement 1991 No 12 and *Law for Business*, January 1992, p. 78.
48 See DTI *Single Market News* No 4 Spring 1992.
49 See *Lawyer's Europe*, Winter 1991, p. 14, and for more details *Single Market Report*, HM Customs & Excise update on 1992, Winter 1991/1992, pp. 1–6.
50 See proposal for a fifth Directive on the structure and management of PLCs, OJ 1983 C 240, pp. 2–38. For a comprehensive review of the harmonization of Company Law see Frank Wooldridge, *European Company Law* (1991).
51 See COM(84) 727.
52 See OJ 1990 C 240, pp. 7–30; see also Frans van Kraay, 'draft directive on company take-overs', *Law for Business* April 1990, pp. 222–4.
53 See Council Regulation No 2137/85, OJ 1985 L 199; for a comment see Frans van Kraay, 'New business co-operation tool; the European interest grouping, *Law for Business* November/December 1989, p. 46 *et seq.*
54 See COM(91) 95 final, p. 28.

55 See answer to parliamentary question OJ 1990 C 283/22.

56 For more details see Frans van Kraay, *Law for Business* November 1991, p. 41.

57 See COM(89) 268 Final and COM(88) 320 and, for a comment on this proposal, see Frans van Kraay, 'What happened to the European Company Statute?', *Law for Business* October 1990, p. 460.

58 See note 1, p. 8.

59 Vlaamse Reisbureaus v. Sociale Dienst 311/85 [1989] 4 CMLR 213.

60 See note 27.

61 Ministère Public v. Asjes, joined cases 209 to 213/84 [1986] ECR 1425.

62 See OJ 1988 L 359/46.

63 For a comment on this measure see Frans van Kraay, 'Franchising agreements', *Law for Business* April 1989, p. 250 *et seq.*

64 OJ 1989 L 395/1. See also Frans van Kraay, 'Agreement on merger rules' JALT 1990, pp. 166–70; Frans van Kraay *ICLQ* 1977 pp. 468–80; Frans van Kraay, *ELRev* 1977, p. 54 *et seq.*; Frank Wooldridge *Law for Business* November 1990, pp. 35–7; Frans van Kraay, 'Towards European merger control legislation, ibid. January 1989, p. 101 *et seq.*, and Frans van Kraay, 'Big business unhappy with merger control rules', ibid. January 1991, pp. 91–2.

65 See *Agence Europe* 10 December 1989, No 5150 (special edition) and Frans van Kraay, *Law for Business* June 1990, p. 324.

66 See COM(90) 228 and Frans van Kraay, *Law for Business* October 1991, p. 425.

67 See note 43, p. 19.

68 See COM(90) 317 and Frans van Kraay, *Law for Business* October 1991, p. 425.

69 See COM(90) 581 and Frans van Kraay, *Law for Business* November 1991, p. 39.

70 See COM(90) 563, Commission information memo p. 93, 28 November 1990 and Frans van Kraay, *Law for Business* January 1992, p. 79.

71 See ISEC/B20/91 22 July 1991.

72 See note 58, p. 9.

73 On the EC's actions relating to SMEs see *inter alia* Frans van Kraay, 'EC enterprise policy and SME's', *Law for Business* November 1991, p. 141 and 'Simple administrative procedures in the EC', ibid. February 1989, p. 57; 'Co-operation between European firms', ibid. March 1989, p. 207 *et seq.*; 'SME management training', ibid. June 1989, p. 349; 'SME action plan', ibid. July 1989, p. 399 *et seq.*; 'Single Member Companies', ibid. March 1990, p. 177; 'Enterprise policy and SME's', ibid. November 1990, p. 47 *et seq.*; 'BC net fully operational', ibid. February 1991, p. 134; 'Administrative simplification in favour of SME's', ibid. April 1991, p. 218; 'Business Cooperation Network', ibid. April 1991, p. 219.

74 See COM(90) 528 and Frans van Kraay, 'Enterprise policy on SME's', *Law for Business*, p. 41.
75 See Frans van Kraay, ibid. February 1989, p. 153.
76 See note 58 p. 9.
77 Ibid.
78 Ibid. and Commission's working paper for the Council meeting on tourism on 29 November 1990; 1990 (SEC) 2356 for more details.
79 See OJ 1990 L 158.
80 See OJ 1991 L 36.
81 See COM(90) 322 final and Frans van Kraay, *Law for Business* May 1991, p. 260.
82 See note 1, p. 10.
83 Regulation 797/85 OJ 1985 L 93/1.
84 See note 1, p. 10.
85 Council Regulation 1820/80, OJ 1980 L 180, p. 1.
86 Council Regulation 1401/86, OJ 1986 128/5.
87 COM(90) 336.
88 See note 1, p. 10, and for further details on EC action in this sphere see COM(90) 430 final 'Community action to promote rural tourism'.
89 See note 1, p. 11 and 'A fresh boost for culture in the European Community', *EC Bull* supp. 4/87.
90 See p. 64.
91 See Resolution of the Ministers responsible for cultural affairs, meeting within the Council on the establishment of transnational cultural itineraries, OJ 1986 C44/2.
92 See *Tourism and Regional Development*, p. 9.
93 See ESC opinion, ENVIREG, OJ 1990 C 112.
94 OJ 1990 C 231/234.
95 See note 87.
96 For more details see Frans van Kraay, *Law for Business* March 1991, p. 177.
97 See D. Lasok, ibid. April 1991, p. 210, and Council Directive 85/337, OJ 1985 L 175.
98 See Directive 76/160 OJ 1976, L 31 and for more details see Chapter 5, p. 91.
99 See, for example: Dir. 76/464, OJ 1976 L 129 on dangerous substances discharged into the aquatic environment; Dir. 73/404, OJ 1973 L 347 on approximation of national law re detergents; Dir. 78/176, OJ 1978 L 54 on waste from the titanium dioxide industry; Dir. 80/779, OJ 1980 L 229 on air quality limit values and guide values for sulphur dioxide and suspended particulates; Dir. 78/611, OJ 1978 L 197 on lead content of petrol.
100 *Agence Europe* 7 June 1990, No 5269.
101 See *Law for Business* February 1991, p. 134.

102 See ibid. June 1991, p. 303.For a concise and succinct article on the EC's environment policy, see D. Lasok, ibid. April 1991, p. 208 *et seq.* and F. van Kraay, *JALT* 1991, Vol. 25, No 2, p. 162 *et seq.*
103 See note 1, p. 12.
104 E.g. COMETT, EUROTECNET, ERASMUS, PETRA, IRIS, FORCE, EUROFORM, LEDA and the ARCHIPELAGO experiment. For more details see the memorandum on the rationalization and co-ordination of vocational training programmes at EC level, COM(90) 334.
105 See Frans van Kraay, *Law for Business*, June 1989, p. 349 and SEC(88) 1860.
106 See *EC Bull* supp. 4/82 and OJ 1984 C 115.
107 See OJ 1986 C 114.
108 See OJ 1986 L 384/54.
109 Ibid. p. 60.
110 OJ 1986 C 340.
111 See note 108, p. 52 for Council Decision establishing a consultation and co-operation procedure in the field of tourism.
112 See Council Decision on an action programme for European Year of Tourism 1990, OJ 1989 L 17.
113 See COM(88) 413 final, p. 1.
114 See OJ 1988 C 49.
115 See note 113, OJ 1988 C 293/12, and OJ 1989 L 17.
116 See note 54.
117 See European File 2/90, p. 5.
118 See COM(91) 95 final.
119 Ibid. p. 2.
120 On financial contributions to the European Song Contest see answers to written question No 2911/90, OJ 1991 C 98/42.
121 See note 118, p. 3.
122 For more details see note 118.
123 See note 1, p. 14.
124 Ibid. p. 15.

4: Actions of particular importance for business and consumers

1 See Council Directive 90/314 on package travel, package holidays and package tours, OJ 1990 L 158/59. For a comment on the proposal for this Directive see Frans van Kraay, *Law for Business* July 1990, p. 373 *et seq.*; for a comment on the Directive see Frans van Kraay, *JALT* 1991, Vol. 25, no 3, p. 266 *et seq.*
2 See Article 4.
3 See Article 4 of the re-examined proposal: OJ 1990 C 158/8.
4 See Commission background report ISEC/B11/88 16 May 1988.
5 See also *Holiday Which* January 1985 and January 1987.

6 See Lyn Julius, 'Let's get the package business tied up', *Europe* September/October 1988, p. 6.
7 See *EC Bull* supp. 4/82.
8 See OJ 1984 C 115.
9 Study undertaken by GFK Marktforschung, Nüremberg; see also note 4, p. 2.
10 See note 6.
11 See OJ 1989 C 102/27.
12 See Council Recommendation on standardized information in existing hotels. OJ 1986 L 384/54.
13 See OJ 1986 C 114/8.
14 See hotel characterization report No I (classification). May 1989, Horwarth & Horwarth (UK) Ltd., section I, Introduction and Background.
15 Ibid. p. 131.
16 See Council Recommendation on fire safety in existing hotels 1986 L 384/60.
17 See PE 146.115/final, p. 21.

5: Latest EC action plan to assist tourism

1 See Community action plan to assist tourism, COM(91) 97 final, Brussels 24 April 1991, p. 15 et seq.
2 Ibid. p. 16 and OJ 1990 L 358/89.
3 See PE 146. 115/final, p. 10.
4 See Chapter 2, p. 42.
5 See note 1, p. 17.
6 Ibid. p. 19 and Resolution of the European Parliament on the measures needed to protect the environment from potential damage caused by mass tourism, as part of European Year of Tourism, OJ 1990 C 231/234. See also Chapter 2.
7 See annex COM(86) 32 final.
8 See note 1, p. 20 and OJ 1988 C 290; OJ 1989 C 256; Pereira Report, EP DOC 144.146.
9 See Directive 84/641 OJ 1984 L 339/21; Directive 73/239 OJ 1973 L 228/3; Directive 76/580 OJ 1976 L 189/13; and for more details see D. Lasok, *The Professions and Services in the European Economic Community*, p. 291 *et seq*.
10 See note 1, p. 22.
11 See COM(90) 438 final.
12 See Chapter 3, p. 64; for more details see note 1, p. 24 *et seq*.
13 See *Tourism and Regional Development*, p. 9.
14 See note 1, p. 26 *et seq*.
15 Directive 76/160, OJ 1976 L 31.

16 For more details see 'The European Blue Flag 1990', FEEE, European Office Denmark.
17 See answer to written question No 1752/90, OJ 1990 C 312/50.
18 For more details see Duccio Guerra, 'Tourism and vocational qualifications', *CEDEFOP News*, No 3 August 1990, p. 2.
19 OJ 1985 L 199/50.
20 See answer to written questions No 1198/89 OJ 1990 C 259/9.
21 See OJ 1989 C 166/1.
22 See OJ 1989 C 209/1.
23 See OJ 1990 L 156.
24 See OJ 1987 L 346 and OJ 1990 C 322.
25 See OJ 1990 C 327.
26 See note 13, p. 21.
27 For more details see COM(91) 95 final, p. 52.
28 Ibid. p. 32.
29 See OJ 1989 L 375.
30 See above Chapter 3, p. 62.
31 See Carlo Ripa di Meana, 'Europe plans new programme to attract American tourists', *Europe* December 1987, p. 28.
32 See written question No 938/90 OJ 1990 C 272/15.
33 See above Chapter 3, p. 66.
34 See note 27, p. 19.

6: Miscellaneous developements

1 See E. McMillan Scott, 'Report on transfrontier property transactions' PE DOC A 3–14/89, p. 9.
2 See petition No 12/87 and for other colourful examples petitions No 104/87; No 292/88 and 196/87.
3 See petition No 124/86 and for more details the report drawn up by the office of the Defensor del pueblo ('Ombudsman') to whom the petition had been referred by the European Parliament, 'Adquisiciones de propriedades Immobiliarias en España' (Españoles y Extranjeros) Madrid, 3 May 1987.
4 See *The Times* 2 July 1991.
5 See Commission answer to parliamentary question 2873/90, OJ 1991 C 136/21 and for the proposal for a Directive on unfair terms in consumer contracts OJ 1990 C 243; see also Frans van Kraay, *Law for Business* May 1991, p. 260.
6 See report on behalf of the legal affairs Committee on the need to fill the legal gap in the timeshare market (Doc A2-199/88 and Resolution of 13 October 1988).
7 See OJ 1985 L 372, p. 31.
8 See Commission report on voting rights in local elections for EC

citizens, *EC Bull* supp. 7/86, COM(86) 487 final and for the text of proposed Directive COM(88) 371 final.

9 See communication from the Commission to the Council on a Council Decision authorizing the Community to participate in negotiations on a Convention on Tourism, COM(88) 586 final.

10 See joint cases 286/82 and 26/83 Luisi and Carbone v. Ministero del Tesoro [1984] *ECR* 377 [1985] 3 *CMLR* 52.

11 OJ 1973, L 172/14.

12 See Diplomatic Conference on the Travel Contract (CCV), Brussels, April 1970 ed. Goemaere, Brussels 1971.

13 See *Unification of Law Yearbook* 1962, pp 96–105.

14 For EC action in this respect see Chapter 2, p. 31.

15 See Chapter 4, p. 74

16 See *Social Europe* supp. 8/89 p 103/4.

7: Conclusion

1 'Travel is the world's biggest industry', *The Times* 19 June 1990.

2 See PE 146.115/final, p. 6.

3 Ibid. p. 9.

4 The Maastricht Treaty has not, as expected and hoped by some, introduced an EC tourism policy as such, but Article 3t does refer to at least measures on tourism.

5 See note 2, p. 28 and PE 137.008.

6 See *Agence Europe* 1 November 1990 No 5362 (new series).

7 See *Tourism and Regional Development*, ESC 1990.

8 Ibid. and *Law for Business* July 1991, p. 345.

9 See note 7, p. 12.

10 See note 7, p. 28.

11 See note 2, pp. 9 and 10.

12 See Chapter 5, p. 82.

13 See Chapter 3.

14 OJ 1989 L 220/1.

15 See note 2, p. 12.

16 OJ 1991 L 36/5.

17 OJ 1989 C 69/213.

18 See note 2, p. 19.

19 Ibid. and see also Chapter 4.

20 See note 2, annex.

21 See note 2, pp. 29 and 30.

22 See note 8, and answer to parliamentary question 2601/90; OJ 1991 C 259/5.

23 See note 8.

24 On the EP's activities see, e.g., EP Resolution on Community policy on tourism, OJ 1984 C 10/281; EP Resolution on facilitation, promotion

and funding of tourism in the EC, OJ 1988 C 49/157; EP Resolution on the measures to protect the environment from potential damage caused by mass tourism as part of the European Year of Tourism, OJ 1990 C 231/234; EP Resolution on the European Year of Tourism 1990, OJ 1991 C 191/238.

25 See PE 146.712, p. 9, EP briefing 10–14 December 1990.

26 For motion for a Resolution by Mr Robles Piquer (Doc. B 3–1092/90) see note 2, annex p. 31.

27 For motion for a Resolution by Mr Denys MEP (DOC B 3–1965/90) see note 2, annex, p. 31.

Bibliography

BOOKS AND ARTICLES

Appels, B., *Kanttekeningen bij de Ontwikkeling van een Europese Richtijn betreffende pakketreizen, met inbegrip van vacantie en Roundreispaketten*, April 1989.

Horwarth & Horwarth, UK Ltd., *Hotel Characterisation* Report I (classification), May 1989.

Julius, Lyn, 'Let's get the package business tied up', *Europe* September/October 1988, p. 6.

Julius, Lyn, 'Don't get burned when you buy a home in the sun', *Kangaroo News*, (1990) 35.

Julius, Lyn, 'Still on our weary way, stumbling blocks to trip up travellers throughout Europe', *Kangaroo News*, (1990), 34, 14–15.

Lasok, D., *The Professions and Services in the European Economic Community*, Kluwer (1986).

McMillan Scott, Edward, *Report of Transfrontier Property Transactions* PE 126.117/final.

McMillan Scott, Edward, *Report of the Committee on Transport and Tourism on a Community Tourism Policy,* PE 146.115/final.

McMillan Scott, Edward, *Report on Facilitation, Promotion and Funding of Tourism*, PE 115.349/final.

Prag, Nicholas, 'Packaging the holiday packages', *Europe*, November/December 1987, 17 *et seq*.

Prag, Nicholas, 'Why tourism is a top priority for a people's Europe', *Europe*, March/April 1989, 3 *et seq*.

Van der Woude, M., and Philip Mead, 'Free movement of the tourist in Community Law' *CML Rev* 25, 117–40.

MISCELLANEOUS EC LITERATURE AND DOCUMENTATION

Draft Convention on the Hotelkeepers Contract, Unidroit, January 1979.
'Initial Guidelines for a Community Policy on Tourism', *EC Bull* supp 4/82.
'Tourism and the Community', *European File* 17/82.
'Council Resolution on a Community policy on tourism', OJ 1984 C 115, 1 *et seq*.
'Community policy on tourism, initial guidelines', OJ (1984) C 115/2.
Tourism: Opinion Economic and Social Committee, February 1984.
ESC Opinion on the draft Council recommendation concerning the adoption of a European emergency health card, OJ 1984 C 206/11.
'Tourism and the European Community', *European File* 11/85.
'Community Action in the Field of Tourism', *EC Bull* supp 4/86.
ESC opinion on Community action in the field of Tourism, OJ 1986 C 328/1.
Resolution of the Council and the representative of the Member States, meeting within the Council, on the adoption of a European emergency health card, OJ 1986 C 184/4.
Proposal for a Council Decision establishing a consultation and coordination procedure in the field of tourism, OJ 1986 C 114/11.
Council Decision establishing a consultation and coordination procedure in the field of tourism, OJ 1986 L 384/52.
'Over 1000 projects in the tourism sector' *EIB Information*, October 1986, 50, 9 *et seq*.
'Community action in the field of tourism', COM(86) 32 final.
Proposal for a Council Recommendation on standardised information on existing hotels, COM(86) 32.
Proposal for a Council Decision establishing a consultation and coordination procedure in the field of tourism, COM(86) 32.
Council recommendation on standardised information in existing hotels, OJ 1986 L 384/54.
Council Recommendation on fire safety in hotels, OJ 1986 L 284/60.
Resolution of the ministers responsible for cultural affairs meeting within the Council on the establishment of transnational cultural itineraries, OJ 1986 C 44/2.
The European Community and tourism, European File 9/87.
EP Resolution on facilitation, promotion and funding of tourism in the EC, DOC C A2–209/87, OJ 1986 C 49/157.

Council Decision establishing a consultation and coordination procedure in the field of tourism, OJ 1987 C7/327.

EP Resolution re Decision establishing a consultation and coordination procedure in the field of tourism, OJ 1987 C7/328.

'Europe plans new program to attract American tourists', *Europe* December 1987, 28 *et seq.*

Communication from the Commission to the Council on a Council Decision authorising the Community to participate in negotiations on a convention on Tourism. COM(88) 586 final.

'A people's Europe', *EC Bull* supp. 2/88.

'Package Travel: protection for the consumer', background report, 16 May 1988, ISEC/B11/88.

'The EC and tourism', *Europe* May 1988, 24 *et seq.*

ESC opinion on the proposal for a Council Directive on package travel, including package holidays and package tours, OJ 1989 C 102/27.

Communication on the comparability of vocational training qualifications between the Member States of the EC established in implementing Council Decision 85/368, Hotel and Catering Industry, OJ 1989 C 166, 1–89.

'Property cheats will face tougher legislation', *EP News* 15 September 1989.

'Tourism in Europe', *Trends 1989*, Eurostat.

'1990 Focus on tourism in the Community'. *EIB Information* 62 (1989) 4 *et seq.*

Preliminary Draft Convention on the Hotelkeepers' contract, Unidroit September 1989.

1990 European Year of Tourism, European File 2/90.

1990 European Year of Tourism ISEC/B9/90, 26 February 1990.

The citizen's Europe advisory service ISEC/B5/90, 25 January 1990.

Proposal for a Council Decision on the implementation of a multiannual programme 1991–1993, for developing community tourism statistics, COM(90) 211 final.

The European Blue Flag 1990, published by FEEE European Office, Denmark.

'Tourism and vocational qualifications', *CEDEFOP News* No 3 August 1990, p. 1 *et seq.*

Tourism and Regional Development Economic and Social Committee Brussels 1990.

Euro Tourism 1990, Année Européenne du Tourisme.

'Tourism', *The Courier*, July/August 1990 pp. 50–5.

Proposal for a Council Decision on an action programme for European Tourism Year 1990, COM(88) 413 final.

Council Decision of 21 December 1988 on an action programme for European Year of Tourism 1990, CES 257/90 final, appendix 2.

Observations of Government and of interested organisations on the preliminary Draft Convention on the Hotelkeepers' Contract, Unidroit, January 1990.

Proposal for a Council Decision on the implementation of a multiannual programme (1991–1993) for developing Community Tourism statistics, OJ 1990 C 150/4.

European Community transport policy in the approach to 1992, European File 9/90.

Community action plan to assist tourism COM(91) 97 final.

Report by the Commission to the Council and the European Parliament on the European Year of Tourism, COM(91) 95 final.

'Umbrella Europe, Campaign for travellers rights in Europe', published by the European Democratic Group of the European Parliament.

'Tourism policy and International Tourism in OECD Member Countries', OECD publications.

Europeans and their holidays, Internal EC Document no VII/165, Commission DG VII.

'The 1992 challenge for the Hotel, Restaurant and Café Industry', HOTREC White paper.

European Year of Tourism, explanatory note.

'The Tourism sector in the Community; a study of concentration, competition and competitiveness', EC Commission.

Table of Legislation

Conventions and Treaties

Table of Cases

Numerical Table

Alphabetical Table

Index